Secrets of a Great Showman

HARRY HOUDINI

Fifty years after his last performance, Houdini is still the world's most famous mystifier. Now, for the first time in paperback, the secrets of the incredible exploits that enthralled the world . . .

Details of spectacular state illusions:

A Vanish in Mid-Air
A Decapitation Act
The Torture Pillory
The Famous Giant Ball of Wool

Plus many more such baffling feats:

· card tricks · slate tricks · platform tricks
· message-reading and second-sight tricks

**THE THRILLING TRICKS
OF THE GREAT MAGICIAN
WHO MYSTIFIED THE WORLD**

Bantam Books by Walter B. Gibson

HOUDINI'S ESCAPES
HOUDINI'S MAGIC

HOUDINI'S MAGIC

PREPARED FROM HOUDINI'S PRIVATE NOTEBOOKS AND
MEMORANDA WITH THE ASSISTANCE OF BEATRICE HOUDINI,
WIDOW OF HOUDINI, AND BERNARD M. L. ERNST,
PRESIDENT OF THE PARENT ASSEMBLY OF THE SOCIETY
OF AMERICAN MAGICIANS

by WALTER B. GIBSON

Introduction by
Milbourne Christopher

BANTAM BOOKS
TORONTO · NEW YORK · LONDON

This low-priced Bantam Book
has been completely reset in a type face
A Bantam Book/published by arrangement with
designed for easy reading, and was printed
from new plates. It contains the complete
text of the original hard-cover edition.
NOT ONE WORD HAS BEEN OMITTED.

HOUDINI'S MAGIC
Funk & Wagnalls Publishing Company, Inc.

PRINTING HISTORY
Originally published by Blue Ribbon Books,
Harcourt Brace in 1932
Funk & Wagnalls edition (part of a two volume book,
HOUDINI'S ESCAPES AND MAGIC) published January 1976
Bantam edition/November 1976

ISBN 0-553-10397-0

Published simultaneously in the United States and Canada

PRINTED IN THE UNITED STATES OF AMERICA

0 9 8 7 6 5 4 3 2 1

INTRODUCTION

by Milbourne Christopher

A new generation, caught up in the biggest magic boom since the heyday of vaudeville, is enthralled by the incredible exploits of Houdini. Books, films, television and radio documentaries, and magazine and newspaper features have presented thrilling, if frequently fanciful, accounts of his feats. This dynamic showman, a critic noted, could get out of manacles quicker than most people get out of bed. No restraining device could hold him; Houdini released himself from welded cylinders, government jails, and submerged iron-banded boxes—without leaving a clue to his methods.

How did "the Elusive American" do it? Sir Arthur Conan Doyle thought he knew. The creator of Sherlock Holmes stated unequivocally that his friend was a powerful medium. How else could he free himself, wrists shackled four feet apart in a position that made it impossible for him to reach a duplicate key, or a lock pick? Conan Doyle also insisted there was no "normal way" for Houdini to penetrate a paper bag or a "sealed glass tank" without ripping the first or smashing the second.

Earlier, J. Hewat MacKenzie, president of the British College of Psychic Science, had been on a London stage when Houdini was locked in an airtight, water-filled container, then enclosed in a curtained cabinet. Moments before the drenched escapologist burst through the drapes, MacKenzie felt a draft. This, he stated, was positive proof that Houdini had dematerialized his body and oozed out.

An explanation for Houdini's escape from a challenge packing crate was advanced by a woman who saw him during a record-breaking nine-month run at Keith's Theatre in Boston. She said Mrs. Houdini, concealed in the cabinet that covered the box, freed him by extracting the nails with a magnet. Another spectator disagreed. In her opinion, the man who came forward to accept the applause was a double. Houdini, she continued, stayed in the crate until his assistants released him after the show.

So much for conjectures. Practical instructions for the box-escapes and the feats Conan Doyle and MacKenzie said were done with psychic aid are to be found in the pages that follow.

Houdini died at the age of fifty-two in Detroit on October 31, 1926. Later, his widow and his lawyer sent stacks of the notes he had made through the years to his friend, Walter B. Gibson. Houdini had written three manuals—*Handcuff Secrets, Magical Rope Ties and Escapes*, and *Paper Magic*; he had hoped to produce more.

It was not an easy task for Gibson, a facile writer and a clever conjurer, to prepare this material for publication. Houdini jotted down not only his own methods, but those of his rivals. Some descriptions were brief and required amplification, others were more extensive and sometimes repetitive. Occasionally a sketch would explain more than pages of text. It is fortunate this work is in print. Some of Houdini's notes, all of which Gibson returned, have since disappeared.

It will soon become apparent to the reader that, though Houdini was daring, he never took an uncalculated risk. He would not accept a challenge unless he was sure he could meet it. He was physically fit, an athlete, and a strong swimmer. Yet his assistants were poised to rescue him if he didn't surface on schedule from an underwater box. A dozen less careful performers have been drowned, or seriously injured, because they attempted this feat without sufficient knowledge, or without taking precautions.

Houdini experimented constantly, striving to make his escapes and his magic more effective. This sustained effort, plus his marvelous showmanship, enabled him to become a legend during his lifetime. Fifty years after his last performance, Houdini still is the world's most famous mystifier.

Contents

Introduction   v

Preface   xiii

Part One. INTRODUCTORY

Houdini's Notes on Magic   2

Part Two. IMPROMPTU TRICKS

Coin Transportation   8
The Magnetic Table   8
The Spooky Ball   9
The Talking Glass   10
Four Coin Assembly   11
Cut and Restored String   15
Balanced Drinking Straw   17
Two from One   17
The Dissolving Knot   18
Vanishing Pocket Knife   20

Part Three. CARD TRICKS

A Good Key Card   24
Half and Half   24
The Traveling Card   25
Card Reading Trick   27
A New Card Box   28
The Imprisoned Card   29
A Spelling Trick   31
Card Counting Trick   32

Part Four. SLATE TRICKS

Slate in Bag 36
Improved Slate Writing 37
Novel Slate Writing 39
Spirit Slate Effect 41
Single Slate Trick 43
Newspaper Test 44

Part Five. MESSAGE-READING

Crystal Gazing Mysteries 48
Sealed Message Reading 54
Sealed Envelope Test 56
A Billet Reading 60

Part Six. PLATFORM TRICKS

Red and Green Silks 66
The Vanishing Glass 67
A Clinging Wand (with Vanish) 69
A Vanishing Wand 71
The Traveling Die 72
With the Linking Rings 74
A Neat Production Tube 75
Perfection Paper Tearing 77
Cone and Egg 78
Houdini's Afghan Bands 81
The Vanishing Table Leg 84

Part Seven. STAGE TRICKS

The Traveling Ball 88
Kellar's Wine and Ribbon 90
Hat Suspension 93
A New Dyeing Tube 94
Ching Ling Foo's Paper Trick 97

A Duck Production   100
Chinese Rice Bowls   102

Part Eight. A SECOND SIGHT ACT

A Second Sight Act   106
The Watch Test   108
The Figure Test to 10,000   110
The Playing Card Test   112
The Slate Test   114
The Book Test   115
The Colored Pencil Test   117
Presentation of the Act   118

Part Nine. STAGE ILLUSIONS

Dunninger's Six Chicks   122
Frame and Cabinet   126
The Cask Illusion   129
A Vanish in Mid-air   132
Sawing a Woman into Twins   136
Sardines in Oil   141
The Transformation Cabinet   145
De Kolta's Illusion   148
The Flight of Venus   151
The Giant Ball of Wool   156
A Vanish from a Ladder   159

Part Ten. SPECIAL STAGE EFFECTS

Living Head Illusion   164
Art and Nature   166
The Decapitation Act   169
The Torture Pillory   174
A Milk Bottle Escape   175

Part Eleven. ANTISPIRITUALISTIC EFFECTS

A Spirit Cabinet   180
The Spirit Knots   182
The Vanishing Chair   184
Spirit Photography   186
A Materializing Cabinet   189
Some Mediumistic Effects   191
A Great Cabinet Act   192

Part Twelve. NOTES ON KELLAR

Kellar's Rope Tie   198
The Cabinet Tie   199
Kellar's Committee Cabinet   202
Notes on Suspension   202
A Kellar Reminiscence   203
Conclusion   206

PREFACE

by Bernard M. L. Ernst

Some of the material used by Mr. Gibson in the following pages was given to me by Houdini for publication before his untimely death in 1926, and more was found and sent to me by Mrs. Houdini in later years. Mr. Gibson had a plethora of material thrust upon him and the very difficult task of selecting only enough items to keep this volume within reasonable bounds. The favorable comment on his earlier work, "Houdini's Escapes," in connection with which he encountered the same difficulty, furnishes confidence that "Houdini's Magic" will please the reading public. As in the earlier work, illusions and effects, now used by professional magicians, are not exposed because of the Canons of Ethics and Standards of The Society of American Magicians, of which the author is a member. With the co-operation of Mrs. Beatrice Houdini, I turned over to Mr. Gibson note books and memoranda, largely in Houdini's own handwriting, which seemed to contain new and original ideas, or new and original methods of presenting old time demonstrations of magic. Marginal notations by Houdini indicated that unique effects and "moves" were contained in his rough manuscripts. These have been translated, at times rewritten and presented in clear and non-technical form, and in many instances supplemented by carefully prepared drawings. An effort has been made to present the notes of a great artist in the manner in which he would have done had he lived, and according to the wish that he expressed before his death. Amateur magicians will find in the book a fund of information and many examples of technique and misdirection for which Houdini, among other things, was famous. Then too, there is now offered the kind of tricks, experiments, and illusions which appealed to the

master. Unfortunately his transcendent showmanship
and personality are gone. My collection of magical
apparatus includes many of the devices and articles
devised and built by Houdini for use in connection with
the items which follow. He tested them all and found
that they would work. Indeed, he followed his rule of
trying them out at least three times before he was satisfied that they were worthwhile. Some of his ideas he
gave to his friends while he lived. Others were set aside
for his projected books. Some effects were described in
meticulous detail. Others were merely sketched in crude
form and their possibilities indicated. I have witnessed
Houdini's demonstrations of many of the "experiments" at the dinner table, in the open air during sum-
mer evenings, and in his private library on 113th Street
in the early morning hours. In his hands all were completely deceptive and extraordinarily mysterious. Frequently he would practice several of the effects and
present them at private entertainments to test their
efficacy. When the reception did not satisfy him he
would destroy his notes and abandon the ideas completely. The memoranda which he kept were of things
considered by him to be of value for use in magic and
are included in this book. Its pages will be of interest
and it is hoped that its contents will furnish pleasant
days and evenings to young and old alike.

New York, February 15, 1932.

Part One

INTRODUCTORY

This section is preliminary
to the actual explanations of the magical
secrets which were found in
Houdini's notes. It discusses the scope
and purpose of the material
which forms this book. It also deals
with Houdini and his
relationship to magic.

HOUDINI'S NOTES ON MAGIC

Houdini's notes on magic cover nearly every phase of the art. They were assembled over a period of many years and they form an interesting collection of varied and unusual ideas—many of which have never before appeared in a work on conjuring.

The author began his study of Houdini's notes nearly three years ago. A preliminary examination showed that a considerable percentage of the material dealt with methods of escape. That material was selected and revised. It was published in book form under the title of *Houdini's Escapes*. Following the appearance of the first volume, the author turned his attention to the notes that pertained to magic. These compose the present book.

The art of the magician is much broader than the art of the escape king. Technically, the man who performs escapes is simply devoting his efforts to a specialized branch of magic. In the usual collection of notes on magic, one would expect to find a few escape tricks. Houdini's collection was, of course, an exception, as he won fame as the world's greatest escape artist. At the same time, Houdini was primarily a magician and he was constantly searching for new methods that could be applied to magic.

Houdini began his career as a professional magician. He had high ambitions to reach the topmost place in his chosen art. While he was still progressing, he realized the possibilities of the escape act and turned his great efforts to its development. The success that he gained is now a matter of history. The name of Houdini grew to world-wide fame. Yet Houdini never lost the desire to perform magic. He still held the ambition which has gripped nearly every magician: to appear with his own show, presenting a series of magical effects from feats of sleight of hand to the largest of stage illusions.

When Houdini was demonstrating his escape from a water-torture cell, nearly twenty years ago, he prefaced that feature with a presentation of the needle trick. Some years later, he went on tour in vaudeville, featuring both the needle trick and the substitution-trunk mystery. He had performed those same effects many years before. They were a connecting link with his early career as a magician.

It was not until two years before his death that Houdini set out with his road show, a two and one-half hour performance devoted chiefly to magic. Many who knew Houdini were amazed at the enthusiasm he displayed in his work. Houdini, the magician, was a dynamo of human energy, constantly preparing new illusions and seeking new ideas in magic.

Houdini's attitude toward magic must be considered in connection with his notes on the subject. As an escape artist, he stood supreme. He kept his methods to himself and jealously guarded his most important secrets. He raised a barrier of permanent silence where his own escapes were concerned. The notes that he made on escapes were planned for practical purposes in connection with his own work.

When magic became his chief aim, Houdini adopted a different attitude. He recognized the fact that there were many clever and competent magicians. His aim was not to establish a new form of mystery. He wished to take his place in the long line of famous magicians who have mystified the public over a period of many years. He exchanged ideas with those who knew the principles of magical deception. He was receptive to the suggestions of those well versed in magic. In cities where he appeared, he invited local magicians to appear upon his stage and present their best tricks. The author took part in one of these performances during Houdini's engagement in Philadelphia.

Houdini's enthusiasm for magic is reflected in his notes on the subject. He sought to adapt old ideas to new uses, to discover methods that would produce startling and unusual effects. While he had a natural leaning toward practicability, he would not abandon an idea simply because its first plans were not entirely satisfactory. Simplicity is the keynote of many of the best tricks and illusions; but many performers have ceased to progress because they have been too content with their old ideas. Houdini was not restrained in that manner. He frequently took chances with tricks that involved the danger of failure. He was determined to get the most out of magic.

Houdini was different from the conventional magician. He lacked the suavity that is frequently cultivated by magicians. His escape work had brought him into contact with difficult situations. He was often at his best when forced to adopt a challenging attitude. He frequently depended upon showmanship in preference to smoothness. He liked tricks that were different; and he appreciated and commended good magic when he saw it performed. He gained many excellent ideas from his associations with other magicians.

It must be remembered that Houdini was a great collector of magical literature and data regarding magic. He was not satisfied with gathering a few workable ideas and devoting all his efforts to commercializing them. He wanted to know all that he could learn about magic. Hence his notes were not confined to restricted phases of the art. He set down numerous ideas which occurred to him. He mentioned tricks that he had seen or about which he had heard. He made notes of conversations with other magicians. As a result, the material in his notes varies from obscure references to detailed instructions supplemented by accurate diagrams.

In preparing these notes for publication, the author was often forced to supply certain details that were not mentioned in the actual notes. Many factors were implied or suggested; these required careful study in order to understand the exact idea. Some tricks were explained chiefly by memoranda. It was necessary to visualize the effect from a consideration of the method. In some instances, the condition was reversed. The notes told how an illusion would appear to the audience, but were meager when it came to the actual explanation. By applying known principles of magic to the particular problems involved, the author has managed to reconstruct these ideas and thus to present them in the finished form.

The reader should bear one point in mind. With his escapes, Houdini was traveling through undiscovered land. The great percentage of his notes on escapes gave his original ideas. With his magic, Houdini was utilizing many known methods of a highly developed art. His notes, like those of any other practical magician, contain effects that were given to him or which depend to a great extent upon some idea previously used by magicians.

The author is positive that many of Houdini's magical ideas were his own originations. Some of them are entirely unlike anything that has previously been used in magic. It is impossible, however, to state exactly what percentage of the tricks was entirely Houdini's, partly Houdini's, or simply methods that he obtained from others. Houdini left these notes with the definite understanding that books should be prepared from them. Some of the material was unquestionably intended for reference alone—not for complete publication—for with the notes were various small manuscripts which bore the names of the authors.

While it is possible that Houdini purchased or obtained the rights to use such manuscript material, the author has chosen to eliminate it. The notes contained so many interesting and worth-while ideas in magic that it was quite possible to form a complete volume without recourse to material that was definitely proprietary. The purpose has been to make the book chiefly dependent upon Houdini's own ideas. Any other items which have crept in were included for two definite reasons: first, because it was evident that Houdini intended to use them; second, because the tricks possess unusual merit.

The entire preparation of the book has been a matter of selective research. Preference was given to those methods which appeared to be Houdini's own, to those which were explained most clearly, and to those which seemed most practical. Where the notes were unquestionably preliminary drafts, the author has not hesitated to include or suggest modifications and improvements which he considered to be obviously essential. This is a course adopted by every qualified writer on magic when he is preparing a work that is based upon original notations and dependent upon rough diagrams.

The book has been divided into convenient sections, which classify various tricks and stage effects. The preparation of the illustrations has been an important item in the completion of the book. Where an idea is simple, but routine is important, drawings are nonessential; but in cases where unusual or complicated devices are employed, illustrations can tell much more than words. This is particularly true of stage illusions. Hence the sections that explain larger tricks are provided with a greater number of drawings.

This book includes pseudopsychic effects which may be classed as magical methods rather than as the tricks of fraudulent mediums. It also contains a few escapes that were not published in the previous volume. It was evident from the first examination of Houdini's notes that the material which they contained would be of great interest to all persons who enjoy the study of magic. The element of originality is present throughout. The author gained this impression upon first examination of Houdini's notes. Since completing the manuscript, that impression has become a definite opinion. The methods which Houdini considered worthy of publication should prove a welcome addition to the literature of magic.

Part Two

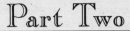

IMPROMPTU TRICKS

Here we have the secrets of
tricks intended for close-up presentation.
These are not numerous,
but they include some very clever
items that will interest all
who present magic of this type.

COIN TRANSPORTATION

An easy trick and an effective one. The magician borrows a coin and two handkerchiefs. He places one handkerchief in an empty glass, crumpling it as he does so. He places the coin in the second handkerchief and inserts it in another glass.

The magician commands the coin to pass from one glass to the other. He lifts the handkerchief that covers the coin. The glass is empty. He lays the handkerchief aside and goes to the other glass. As he draws out the handkerchief, the coin falls into the glass.

The best coin to use is a half-dollar. A duplicate is required. The duplicate coin has a white thread attached to it; on the end of the thread is a small hook. The magician has this coin concealed in his hand. He borrows the handkerchiefs and a half-dollar. Returning to his table, he shows the duplicate half-dollar and lays it with one handkerchief. He crumples the other handkerchief, leaving the borrowed coin in it.

He puts the threaded half-dollar in a glass with the handkerchief over it, at the same time attaching the hook to the center of the handkerchief. When the handkerchief is lifted by the center, the coin dangles beneath it and is not seen. The handkerchief is placed upon the table, the hook being detached so that the coin drops behind some small article.

It is only necessary to draw out the crumpled handkerchief and the borrowed coin will fall into the glass. It is immediately returned, with the handkerchiefs.

THE MAGNETIC TABLE

This is a surprising trick, which may be used as an impromptu stunt or as an effect of pseudopsychic nature. The magician seats himself beside a card table. He raises the table once or twice; then he moves away and the table begins to follow him.

The secret is a piece of black thread, attached to two black pins. The thread is less than a foot in length; the pins are slightly bent.

Seated at the table, the magician attaches the pins to his trousers, one at each knee, the thread passing between. He moves his knees apart as he raises the table and he sets one leg of the table within the line of the thread. As he makes passes with his hands, he slides backward in his chair. In conclusion, the magician detaches the thread and lets it fall to the floor.

This is the same method as that used in the balanced cane; hence the two tricks may be worked on the same occasion. The cane is set upright in front of the performer so that it leans against the thread and remains balanced. The moving table is a spookier trick, however, and is less likely to be detected.

A SPOOKY BALL

While this trick has been described in print and is known to many persons interested in magic, it is included here because Houdini's notes add an effect that gives the trick a most surprising finish.

The trick is best performed on a dinner table. The magician exhibits a steel ball-bearing that measures about one inch in diameter. He places the ball on the table and makes mysterious passes toward it. Slowly the ball begins to roll away across the table. It stops and advances at the magician's command.

The magician lays a lady's handkerchief in front of the ball. The ball rolls along the tablecloth and on to the handkerchief. The magician seizes the four corners of the handkerchief and raises it while the ball is still rolling. He gives the handkerchief and the ball for immediate examination.

A simple apparatus is utilized—a small thin ring attached to a thread. The ring is under the tablecloth. The thread goes to an assistant at the opposite side of the table. The magician lays the ball on the hidden ring. When the assistant pulls the thread, the ball moves across the table, away from the magician. The assistant is apparently an interested onlooker. Every one is intent upon watching the ball in its course.

The added effect is the rolling of the ball into the handkerchief. This is simplicity itself; the weight of the ball enables it to do the trick automatically. The lifting of the handkerchief is the assistant's clue to pull the ring completely away from beneath the tablecloth.

THE TALKING GLASS

A glass, a thread, and a pencil are the required articles. The thread is tied in a loop. The glass is slipped into the loop. The glass should have tapering sides so that it does not slide completely through the loop. The glass is partly filled with water. The other end of the thread is tied about the pencil. The pencil is raised and the glass hangs suspended by the thread. When persons ask questions, the glass responds. It rings softly and in this manner counts to required numbers or answers ques-

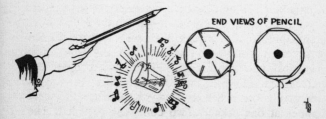

TWISTING THE PENCIL MAKES THE STRING CLIMB.

tions "yes" and "no," one ring signifying the affirmative, two rings the negative.

The pencil used in the trick is hexagonal. The loop is tied about it rather firmly. When the pencil is revolved slowly, the thread begins to climb; then it slips and drops back with a slight jerk, owing to the weight of the glass. This is scarcely observable, especially as the glass is swaying slightly. But each time the string drops, the vibration causes the glass to ring.

If a thin glass is used and the right quantity of water is in the glass, the sound will be quite clear. The proper type of glass can be discovered by experiment. The trick is very effective when performed in a dim light, so that the twisting of the pencil cannot be observed. The performer should center his gaze upon the glass. The sound comes from the glass and this heightens the deception.

FOUR-COIN ASSEMBLY

This is an excellent impromptu trick. It requires a certain amount of skill, but is less difficult than a pure sleight-of-hand demonstration, as the misdirection is well arranged and every movement is completely covered.

To the audience, the trick appears as follows: The magician borrows four coins, all alike. He lays a handkerchief upon the table. He weights down the corners of the handkerchief by placing a coin upon each corner. He takes two pieces of paper, each about four inches square, and covers two of the coins, one with each sheet.

He picks up a loose coin and places it beneath the handkerchief with his right hand. A snap of the fingers —the coin is gone. The empty right hand lifts the sheet of paper at one corner. Two coins are revealed. The coin has apparently joined its mate. The sheet of paper is replaced above the two coins. Another loose coin is magically passed beneath it. Now there are three coins beneath one sheet of paper; one coin beneath the other. At the magician's command, the single coin passes to join the three. The papers are lifted. The four coins have assembled!

The first deception occurs when the performer is explaining what he intends to do. Having put the four coins at the corners of the handkerchief, he exhibits the two sheets of paper, holding one in each hand, fingers beneath, thumb above.

"When I cover the coins nearest me," says the magician, suiting the words with the action, "you see the coins that are farthest away." He lifts the papers and holds them over the other two coins. "When I cover the coins farthest away from me, you see those that are nearest to me."

It is at this point that the performer makes his first movement. The right hand is holding the paper above the coin at the outer right corner. The second finger presses against the lower part of the coin. The right forefinger raises the edge of the coin. Thus the coin is clipped between the fingers, at the back of the hand. Only the fingers are out of sight beneath the paper. The open palm is clearly seen. There appears to be no chance for deception.

The magician raises the left-hand paper from the coin that it is covering. He brings the left hand over to the right. As the left paper covers the right paper, a few inches above it, the right hand drops its paper and takes the paper that the left hand is holding. During this movement, the right fingers are constantly concealed from view. The right hand places the paper that it has taken upon the coin at the lower left corner. It holds the paper there and still retains the coin. The left hand points at both sheets of paper, while the magician remarks: "When I cover the coins diagonally, the other two coins are visible."

The right hand, still carrying its hidden coin, moves

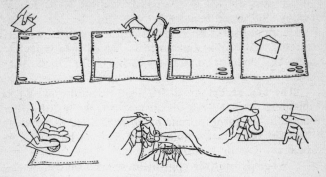

Top, HOW THE TRICK APPEARS.
Bottom, CLIPPING FIRST COIN—TRANSFER OF
EACH "PASSING" COIN—COIN CONCEALED
WHEN PAPER IS TRANSFERRED.

to the upper left corner and covers the coin there. It drops the paper and leaves the coin beneath it. Then both hands point to the coins at the lower corner and the magician says: "I shall use the coins that are nearest to me."

He picks up the coin at the lower left corner, lifting it with the right hand. The left hand raises the corner of the handkerchief. The left fingers are beneath the corner. The right hand slowly slides its coin under the handkerchief. In so doing, it transfers the coin to the left hand, which clips it between the first and second fingers, at the back; just as the right hand previously clipped a coin.

The right hand continues a bit beneath the handkerchief. Then the fingers are snapped. The right hand comes back. It is shown entirely empty. The right hand picks up the paper at the upper left corner of the handkerchief. Two coins are seen there. The left hand is still holding the corner of the handkerchief. The right hand brings the paper over to the left hand. The left moves away from the handkerchief and takes the sheet of

13

paper. This transfer completely covers the coin that is held behind the left hand.

The right hand, being free, moves to the right to take the coin at the lower right corner. The left hand quietly lays the paper upon the two coins at the upper left corner. It leaves its clipped coin beneath the paper and comes back to the lower left corner of the handkerchief. As the left hand lifts the corner of the handkerchief, the magician repeats his previous move. He puts the right hand beneath the cloth. The left fingers clip the coin. The right hand comes out empty. It lifts the sheet of paper at the upper left corner and shows three coins. It transfers the paper to the left hand, which drops the corner of the cloth. The left hand puts the paper upon the three coins, leaving the fourth coin with them. The right hand points to the sheet of paper at the upper right corner of the handkerchief.

The last transfer should be done as mysteriously as possible. The spectators think that there are three coins beneath one sheet of paper and one coin beneath the other. As a matter of fact, all four coins are under one sheet of paper. The magician makes the most of this situation. He commands the last coin to pass and makes a motion with his fingers. He lifts the paper at the upper left corner, with the left hand. This reveals the four coins. The right hand lifts the paper at the upper right corner and shows that the coin has gone. Coins, papers, and handkerchief may be thoroughly examined by the spectators.

If this trick is done properly, the keenest observer will be mystified. The entire routine is natural; the magician is always one step ahead of the onlookers. There should be no great speed. The trick is most effective when done deliberately, as the sleights may be accomplished without fumbling. With a reasoanble amount of practice, this becomes a fine mystery, suitable for close-up presentation.

CUT AND RESTORED STRING

New versions of the cut and restored string trick are constantly appearing. Like so many others, this one has points of novelty that will be of interest to magicians. It possesses that degree of difference which makes it deceptive.

The string used is about two feet in length. The magician measures off three or four inches and holds the string at that point, between his left thumb and forefinger. The right hand takes the long end of the string and weaves it between the left fingers: over the first, under the second, over the third, under the little finger. He winds the string around the little finger a few times; brings it over the little finger, under the third, then over the second and under the forefinger, letting the long end extend.

He picks the spot where the string passes over the second finger (on its return journey) as the approximate center of the string. He clips the string at that place. Then, drawing the string from his fingers, he shows it to be fully restored!

This trick depends upon a very subtle manipulation. It should be noted that the string, on its return journey, apparently crosses the knuckles of the little finger and the center finger, the back of the hand being upward. But the string does not go over the second finger. When his right hand draws the string under the third finger of the left hand, it is hidden from view. It picks up the short end of the string (which is still downward between the left thumb and forefinger) and brings the short end over the second finger of the left hand. The long string passes clear under the second finger of the left hand and also under the first finger. It extends between the left thumb and forefinger. Thus there is just a tiny end over the second finger and that end is clipped

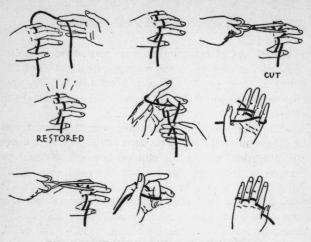

THE ILLUSTRATIONS SHOW THE THREADING AND CUTTING OF THE STRING—ALSO HOW THE SHORT END IS DOUBLED BACK.

between the second finger and the forefinger. Yet it appears to be the center of the entire string.

The magician uses a pair of scissors to clip the string at the point designated. When he draws the string from the left hand, the short end is retained between the fingers and is later dropped on the floor.

This is a good version of the cut and restored string, as it is almost impossible for any one to note the switch. It should be practiced carefully until the performer can weave the string in a natural, easy fashion. Once the idea is fully understood, the trick presents very little difficulty. It is advisable to start slowly with the weaving, to show that everything is fair. The left fingers should be spread after the cutting, to let the string pull free; at the same time, care should be taken to retain the bit of string that was cut from the short end.

BALANCED DRINKING STRAW

The feat of balancing a drinking straw depends upon a neat bit of deception. Any straw may be used. The straw is set upon the tips of the first two fingers, which are held together. The palm of the hand is upward. There the straw remains, balanced.

The secret is an ordinary pin, which the performer has in readiness. It may be kept in the lapel of the coat until needed. The pin is clipped between the first two fingers of the hand. The hand is turned downward, the pin projecting inward. The other hand receives the straw. As the hands approach, the pin is pointed upward as the hand is turned over. The straw is placed over the pin. A careful balance is made and the pin easily keeps the straw in position. It appears to be a bit of skillful jugglery.

In conclusion, the hand is turned slightly and the straw is taken by the free hand. The fingers are opened to allow the pin to fall to the floor; where it will not be noticed.

TWO FROM ONE

This is a neat knot trick with a large handkerchief— preferably a silk handkerchief. The secret is little known. Houdini used the trick in his show, in connection with a series of handkerchief tricks. The handkerchief is tied in a single knot; the magician shakes the handkerchief and two knots appear at different parts of the handkerchief.

It is simply a case of tying two knots in one. The drawings illustrate the method. While one hand holds the end of the handkerchief, the other hand loops the

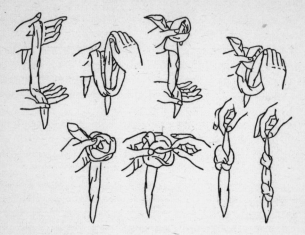

**SLOW MOTION ILLUSTRATION OF THE DOUBLING KNOT.
NOTE THE FORMATION OF EACH LOOP
AND HOW THE TWO ARE ARRANGED TO APPEAR
AS A SINGLE KNOT.**

center once and then again. The knot is tied by thrusting the end of the handkerchief through the double loop. It looks like a single knot when drawn fairly tight.

To make the two knots separate, the handkerchief is held by the upper end and given a quick snap. One knot jumps down the handkerchief. Both knots tighten, and to the observer, the magician has made one knot break apart and form two. The movements of tying should be practiced until they can be performed quickly and naturally.

THE DISSOLVING KNOT

The old dissolving-knot trick is simple but difficult to follow. The magician twists a handkerchief and appar-

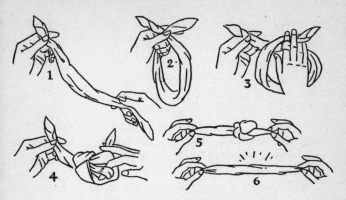

I-2-3, FORMATION OF THE DISSOLVING KNOT.
4, DRAWING A LOOP IN THE CENTER.
5-6, PULL ENDS TO MAKE KNOT VANISH.

ently ties a fair knot in its center. But the knot is not, as
the saying goes. The handkerchief comes out knotless.

The move is as follows: Hold the ends of the handkerchief, one in each hand. Bring the right end over the
left hand and under the knuckles so that it points upward, in front of the loop. Push it through the loop
from above. Pull the end with the right hand and away
goes the knot. It is never formed at all.

The improvement includes the following movement.
Cross the ends of the handkerchief so that the end on
top projects to the right. The left hand takes the left
end. The second and third fingers of the right take the
right end. The right forefinger reaches through the loop.

The finger can then grip a point near the center of
the handkerchief and draw it upward through the loop.
This is facilitated if the left fingers assist. The right
thumb and forefinger pull the center of the handkerchief so that a false knot is formed when the ends are
tightened.

The handkerchief is exhibited in this condition and
the false knot adds to the illusion that the magician has

tied a genuine single knot. When the ends are drawn, the false knot comes out and the handkerchief is seen to be untied after all.

VANISHING POCKETKNIFE

The magician can use a borrowed pocketknife in this trick. He opens the blade of the knife and places the instrument in his left hand, from which it immediately vanishes.

A dull knife-blade is used to aid in this vanish. A

SHOWING KNIFE AND DUPLICATE BLADE WITH LOOP.
ALSO HOW KNIFE IS CARRIED AWAY
WHILE BLADE IS EXHIBITED INSTEAD.

piece of catgut or thin white thread is fitted to the extra knife-blade, at the lower end. The loop is put over the left thumb. The blade hangs out of sight behind the left hand. The magician keeps the palm of the hand toward the spectators.

He asks for an opened knife. He takes it in his right hand and closes the blade while he steps away from the spectators. He lets the onlookers get a glimpse of the handle as he brings the right hand over to the left. Under pretense of squeezing the knife between his hands, he brings the false blade into his left hand. The right hand moves away, carrying the real knife. The left hand lets the false blade come into view, thus giving the impression that it holds the knife. The magician pockets the knife. He brings his hands together and with a rubbing motion forces the hanging blade in back of the left hand. Both hands are opened and the palms are held toward the spectators. The knife has vanished. The false blade is later removed from the left hand.

Part Three

CARD TRICKS

The card tricks found in
Houdini's notes are of various types.
There was very little reference
to sleight of hand. Most of the tricks
required only simple manipulation
or depended upon special
forms of apparatus. The reader will
find some novel effects
with cards in this section.

A GOOD KEY CARD

Magicians who perform card tricks know the value of a "key" card in a pack which is otherwise unprepared. Many clever tricks can be performed with such a card. When a chosen card is taken from the pack, the magician can find his key and cut the pack at that spot for the return of the selected card. The chosen card can be obtained later by finding the key.

This key card is prepared by taking any card from an ordinary pack, dampening it, and peeling it in half. (Playing-cards are in two layers, glued together.) A thin piece of silk is inserted between the portions of the card, and the front and back are glued together. The prepared card is kept under a heavy weight for two or three days. It then bears no signs of preparation that can be ordinarily noticed. But the performer can detect the card at any time and can use it as a key card. It is stiffer and heavier than the other cards in the pack and can be located by riffling the end of the pack.

HALF AND HALF

This is an interesting variation of an older trick, in which a chosen card appears in the magician's pocket. The mystery in this instance is quite different, inasmuch as the magician apparently causes a card to pass from one half of a pack to the other.

A spectator shuffles a pack of cards and divides it in half. He gives one half to the magician. The spectator notes a card in his own half, remembering its distance from the top—for instance, the jack of clubs, eight cards from the top of his half.

The magician then asks the number from the top, referring to the card in the spectator's half. The answer is, "eight." The magician counts off seven cards from his own heap and calmly places the eighth card in his pocket. He palms it, however, and secretly adds it to his half of the pack upon removing his hand from his pocket. The observers believe that the magician has left the eighth card of his own heap in his pocket.

The magician now asks for the spectator's half. In taking it, he places his thumb below the pack and draws off the bottom card. He slaps his hand upon the pack, telling the spectator to hold the pack tightly between his hands. The magician has secretly added a card to the top of the spectator's half.

The spectator now counts down to the eighth card and is told to remove it, the magician taking the remaining cards from him. When the spectator looks at the face of the eighth card, he is surprised to see that it is not the card he selected!

At this point, the magician palms the top card from those that are in his hand. It is the card which the spectator selected. Reaching in his pocket, the magician produces the card and shows his pocket otherwise empty.

The effect is that the *eighth* card of the magician's half changed places with the *selected* (eighth) card of the spectator's half of the pack. While this is a trick requiring sleight of hand, the movements are not difficult. The principal requirement is good patter, convincing showmanship.

THE TRAVELING CARD

A card is selected by the audience. It is placed in a clip on the front of a small stand. The magician shows an envelope. He lets the audience examine it and mark it. The envelope is sealed. The card is taken from the clip and the envelope is placed there instead.

The card is now inserted in another envelope. The

magician strikes the envelope and immediately shows it empty. He tears the envelope into tiny pieces, leaving no doubt regarding the disappearance of the card. He shows his hands empty and picks up the sealed envelope from the clip. He tears open the envelope and brings out the card.

A mechanical stand answers this problem. The original card is forced. There is a duplicate card flat on the stand behind the clip. It is attached to a short lever, which has a spring and is actuated by pressure upon the clip.

The sealed envelope is not faked. It is actually marked and put in the clip after the forced card has been taken by the magician. The envelope in which he places the card has a slit near the flap. The magician is holding the pack. He rests the envelope on the pack as he inserts the chosen card. He pushes it right through the horizontal slit, so that it joins the pack. The envelope may then be shown empty and destroyed.

To produce the duplicate card in the sealed envelope,

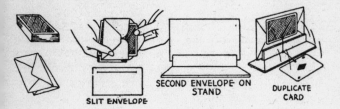

DRAWING SHOWS SLIT ENVELOPE,
THROUGH WHICH CARD IS PUSHED. ALSO SPECIAL STAND
WITH DUPLICATE CARD SNAPPING UP BEHIND ENVELOPE.

the magician simply presses the clip. This causes the lever to rise, so that the duplicate card is in back of the sealed envelope. In taking the sealed envelope from the stand, the magician grips the card also. He cuts the end of the envelope and pretends to draw the card from it. In reality, he draws the card from in back of the envelope.

This mechanical stand is an ingenious idea and is undetectible. Houdini's notes indicate that the trick is intended for several cards—all forced. Each card can be placed in a separate envelope. At the finish, all are found in the marked envelope. They all come up together in the clip end of the lever. The base of the clip hides the duplicate cards prior to the operation of the lever. The sealed envelope is considerably larger than a playing-card.

CARD READING TRICK

A pack of cards is given to the audience. The cards are thoroughly shuffled. Various spectators take cards and place them in envelopes—a card to each envelope. The envelopes are sealed. They are placed in a hat.

HOW CARDS CAN BE READ THROUGH
SEALED ENVELOPES PLACED IN A HAT.

Upon the platform the magician removes an envelope from the hat. He holds the envelope to his forehead. He names the card within it. He tosses out the envelope. It is opened and the card is identified. This is repeated with the remaining envelopes.

The envelopes are thin. The playing cards are of a special type, also very thin. Neither the envelopes nor the cards are ordinarily transparent, but they are thin enough to become so under the glare of a light.

The magician works with considerable light about him. He secretly places a small pocket flashlight in the hat after he receives it, and turns on the light. As he removes each envelope he holds it directly above the glare of the electric torch. The card can then be distinguished through the texture of the envelope.

The reason that the magician chooses a well-lighted position is to overcome the glare of the flashlight. He keeps the mouth of the hat turned toward himself as he removes the envelopes. The holding of each envelope so that it rests against the forehead is merely a bit of byplay intended to mislead the audience.

This principle may be applied to the reading of sealed questions. Where questions are used, the magician supplies very thin cards and can use envelopes that are fairly thick. No spectator can read his own card through the envelope; hence there is no reason to suppose that the magician can read the question.

An effective part of this trick is the immediate returning of each envelope to its owner. Every envelope is given back sealed and the spectators wonder how the trick is possible. The placing of the light in the hat is by no means a difficult matter. A small flashlight is easily palmed and the magician has plenty of opportunity to insert it while he pretends to arrange the envelopes in a pile inside the hat.

A NEW CARD BOX

The familiar card box is simply a mechanical box in which a card appears through the aid of a falling flap. This trick is a variation of the card box, with a different ending. The magician states that he will make a chosen card appear in an empty box. He invites some one to stand beside him and hold the box, which is shown to contain nothing.

The card is vanished by the magician, but when the

box is opened it is still empty. The magician begins a
conference with the person who held the box. In talking, they turn their backs to the audience and the
chosen card is seen attached to the back of the volunteer assistant.

This trick is done with the aid of the card box. The
box is actually empty, but it has a double bottom on the
outside. There is a thin space between the bottoms.
This holds an inserted card. The card has a projecting
hook.

When the magician gets the box, he holds it in his
right hand, and in pointing with his left, he holds attention while he presses the box against his assistant's
back. By simply drawing away the box, the magician
leaves the card on the person's back. The box is then
shown empty and the trick is ready for its conclusion.
The card that is vanished is a duplicate of the one on
the assistant's back.

THE IMPRISONED CARD

A card is chosen from a pack. It is placed in a prison,
namely, a thin oblong box, fitted with crossbars, just
large enough to receive the card. The magician also
exhibits an envelope. He shows that the envelope is
large enough to hold the entire box. He seals the envelope and throws a handkerchief over the box. When
he removes the cloth, the card is gone from its prison.
Every one can see through the spaces between the slats.
The card is found in the envelope.

The box that is used has special slides behind the
slats. These fall into place when the box is inverted, so
that they fill the spaces between the slats. The slides are
portions of a playing-card; they duplicate the card that
is used in the trick.

The box is first held upright; the opening into which
the card is inserted points upward. The real card is put

in. It goes behind the slides. The back of the box is shown and the back of the real card is seen there. At this moment, the box is inverted; the slides come down, but their movement is not seen because of the card.

Turning the box to show the front, the magician picks up the envelope and shows it empty. He starts to put the box in the envelope but does not do so. At this

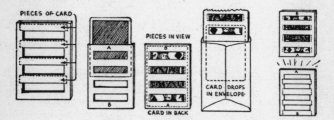

CONSTRUCTION OF SPECIAL BOX FOR VANISHING THE CARD. NOTE HOW SECTIONS OF CARD SLIDE FROM SLATS; ALSO HOW GENUINE CARD IS SECRETLY DROPPED IN ENVELOPE.

point, he releases the genuine card. It falls into the envelope. Its progress is invisible because of the presence of the front slides, which cover it. The envelope is sealed. The box is covered with a handkerchief. It is inverted beneath the cloth. The slides go back out of view. The box will now appear empty.

The magician removes the handkerchief in a suspicious manner. He shows the box empty from both sides and lays it on the table. Every one suspects that the card is in the handkerchief. The magician appears annoyed for a time; finally he shows that the handkerchief is empty. In fact, he passes it out for examination.

This puzzles the spectators, as they no longer have any suspicion of the box. A member of the audience is allowed to open the sealed envelope, and when the chosen card is found therein, the trick arrives at its surprising conclusion.

A SPELLING TRICK

A spectator removes a card from a pack. He looks at the card and places it in his pocket. The pack is handed to the man and he is told to spell the suit of his card, dealing a card from the top of the pack as he names each letter. For instance: S-P-A-D-E-S—six cards. He must turn up the final letter of his spelling. The card proves to be of the suit he spelt. Continuing from that point, he spells the value of the card, as Q-U-E-E-N; when he turns up the last card, it proves to be a queen —or whatever value he named.

This trick depends upon an arrangement of the cards. There are eighteen cards on top of the pack, in the following order:

three of hearts	eight of spades
queen of spades	king of hearts
seven of hearts	three of spades
deuce of spades	queen of hearts
eight of hearts	seven of spades
knave of spades	deuce of hearts
knave of hearts	eight of clubs
ten of spades	knave of clubs
four of hearts	knave of diamonds

Note that the two-spot is called the "deuce," while a jack is referred to as a "knave." This is in accordance with the sytem found in Houdini's notes.

The routine is as follows. Cut the pack, bringing the pre-arranged group to the center. Spread these cards so that the spectator will take one of the top seven of the special group. When he takes the card, immediately cut the pack at that point so that the card below the card removed becomes the top card of the pack. This is done by separating the halves of the pack and it is so natural that no one will ever notice it. The pack is scarcely considered at all, as the spectator still has his card, which he notes and places in his pocket.

The pack is given to the spectator and he is instructed how to spell—first the suit, then the value. The arrangement of the cards makes the last card of the first spelling show the suit, while the last card of the second spelling reveals the value.

This is an unusual idea and it has possibilities of greater development. The individual performer can work out his own system if he chooses to do so. With the cards properly arranged, the trick is automatic.

CARD COUNTING TRICK

The magician borrows a pack of cards. A spectator shuffles the pack. The magician demonstrates how he wants the spectator to count down to a certain number, look at the last card dealt, and place the pack upon the little pile of cards. Having explained this, the magician writes the name of a card upon a piece of paper and folds the paper. He goes away while the spectator counts to any number he wishes, looks at the last card dealt, and drops the pack on top. The pack is then cut several times. The magician does not know the number to which the person counted.

Now the pack is given to a second party. The first person whispers to that person the number that he dealt. Meanwhile the magician writes something on a second slip of paper. The second person takes the pack and counts down to the same number as the first person. He looks at the card last dealt. When the slips of paper are opened, they are found to bear the names of the cards that were chosen by the spectators!

This is a very neat trick, yet it depends upon a

comparatively simple routine. Before the counting, the magician receives the shuffled pack. He secretly bends up the inner left corner of the top card, which serves as a "key" from then on. In spreading the cards from hand to hand, the magician carelessly demonstrates that the suits are well mixed. This gives him a chance to turn up the lower corner of the seventh card from the top and to note its index. This corner is allowed to fall back after it has been turned far enough to note the value of the card. We will suppose that the card is the ace of hearts.

Turning the pack face down, the magician says: "I want you to count off any number—say five—dealing the cards one by one." He suits these words with the action. Holding the fifth card, he adds: "Look at the last card you deal, drop it on those already dealt and put the pack on the heap." He also demonstrates this. The counting has reversed the order of the five top cards. The key card is now on the bottom of the pack. The known card (ace of hearts) is second from the top.

The magician writes "ace of hearts" on a slip of paper. He marks the paper with the figure 2. He folds the paper so that no one can see what he has written. A spectator now deals to any number—let us suppose ten—looks at the tenth card dealt, and drops the pack on top of the heap. Suppose the tenth card is the four of clubs. After the deal and the placement of the pack, the key card is upon the four of clubs.

The pack is now cut several times. The magician makes the final cuts. This enables him to cut the pack at his key card and to bring the key to the top of the pack. He carelessly lifts the two top cards of the pack. He glimpses the four of clubs, which is directly below the key card, namely, the second card from the top. He hands the pack to the second spectator. On a piece of paper he writes "four of clubs" and marks the paper with the figure 1. He folds the paper. Now the first man whispers the number he counted—ten—to the second man, who deals ten cards. The last one dealt is the one he looks at. It will be the ace of hearts.

The magician hands the slips to the spectators. They open the papers and find that the predictions are correct, that the performer has written down "four of clubs" and "ace of hearts" and has numbered the slips 1 and 2, respectively. This is a most bewildering result.

Note that the slips are numbered in reversed order. They should be handled rather carelessly when they are picked up so that no one remembers which was the slip first written. The spectators naturally suppose that the slip marked 1 was the first slip and the slip marked 2 was the second.

This trick should be rehearsed with the actual cards, and with a little practice its details can be learned thoroughly. Note that each deal reverses the order of the cards dealt; that the last card dealt is the one looked at; that it is laid on the heap dealt and the pack is put over all. Cutting the pack does not disturb the rotation of the cards.

If the magician is using his own pack of cards, he can have a key card—either the familiar "short card" or a key of the type described elsewhere in this section on card tricks. With a key card, the magician simply cuts the pack after it has been shuffled, thus bringing the key to the top. He uses the key in place of the bent corner that is necessary with the unprepared pack. When the bent corner is used, the bend should be sharp enough to enable the performer to locate the card by simply looking at the corner of the pack.

Part Four

SLATE TRICKS

Houdini made a specialty of
all tricks of a pseudopsychic nature.
The slate tricks which he
mentioned in his notes are both practical
and novel. Most of them are
specially suited to magical presentation.

SLATE IN BAG

This is a unique slate-writing effect that may be presented as a duplication of mediumistic methods. A slate is placed in a large cloth bag. The bag is tied or sewed

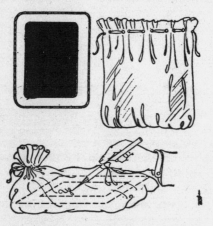

**THE SHARP SLATE PENCIL IS PUSHED
THROUGH THE CLOTH OF THE BAG.**

so firmly that there is no opportunity to open it. The bag and its seals are marked—the slate may also be marked.

The performer then retires to a cabinet or leaves the room. Upon his return, he delivers the bag intact to the spectators. When the bag is opened, writing is discovered on the slate. Everything stands complete examination.

The only special feature of the bag is the type of material used. A dark-colored baize is suitable, although some other coarse cloth will do. The performer has a slate pencil that is sharpened to a point. The bag is much larger than the slate. The performer squeezes the cloth and takes up a fold. He pushes the point of the pencil through the material and writes the message with the point. He then replaces the slate pencil in his pocket.

Carefully done, this leaves no telltale mark on the cloth of the bag. Both the bag and the slate can be thoroughly examined before and after the trick, for there is no substitution of either slate or bag; nor are the knots or seals touched in any way.

IMPROVED SLATE-WRITING

The trick of producing a written message upon a slate is one which magicians have often used. The standard method involves two slates, which are cleaned, placed together, and held for a few moments. When the slates are separated, a message has appeared upon one or both of the slates.

The usual apparatus is a "flap" or thin piece of material. This may be made of a silicate or of black fiber. It fits within the rim of one slate and appears to be the surface of the slate itself. The message is written on that surface of the slate which is covered by the flap. When the slates are placed together and turned over, the flap falls. Thus the message is revealed when the slates are separated.

With an ordinary flap of this type, the slates cannot be examined unless some method is used to dispose of the flap. If this is done, the slates can be inspected after the trick is over. It was Houdini's idea to present a slate trick in which the slates would be examined *before* the message appeared; then to repeat the trick by obtaining a second message.

To accomplish this, he devised a special box into which the slates could slide, the box being open at one

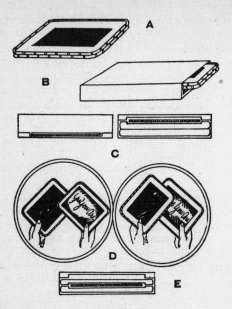

A, TWO EXAMINED SLATES. B, SLATES SLID IN BOX.
C, NOTE HOW FLAP DROPS FROM BOX TO SLATE, WHEN
BOX IS INVERTED. D, SLATES SHIFTED WITHOUT
SHOWING MESSAGE. E, FLAP FALLS BETWEEN SLATES
WHEN THEY ARE REPLACED IN BOX.

end. The box is of flat construction, just large enough
to receive the slates. It appears to be simply a carrying
case for the slates.

The slates are slid from the box and are given for
examination. They are pushed back into the box. In the
lower surface of the box is a depression that holds a
flap. There is writing on both sides of the flap. After the
slates are pushed in, the box is turned over. The flap
drops upon the slate that is then uppermost. The performer tilts the box toward himself and removes the
slates. He separates them and pretends that he sees no
writing. He puts the slates together again; in so doing,

he alters their position so that the writing (on the flap) is between the slates. He replaces them in the box. Upon removal, the writing is discovered on the inner surface of the lower slate.

Before the audience has an opportunity to pick up the slates, the performer takes a damp cloth and wipes out the message which he has revealed. He puts the slates together and replaces them in the box. He turns over the box in raising it. The flap drops from one slate to the other. Now, when the slates are separated a second message has appeared on the inner surface of the lower slate. It is the reverse side of the flap which bears the message.

This is shown; the message is erased and the slates are again replaced in the box, which is turned so that the flap falls into its original depression. The performer then proceeds with another trick. Should any one demand to see the slates, they can be taken from the box and given for inspection. The inside of the box is painted black, so that the flap—without its writing—is invisible at the conclusion.

This is a highly effective routine that possesses puzzling features. Needless to say, a great deal of its effectiveness depends upon well-planned presentation.

NOVEL SLATE-WRITING

This is an improvement on a slate-writing trick. To understand its usefulness, we must first consider a very clever method of spirit slate-writing which was first explained more than thirty years ago.

The magician has a large thimble which fits upon his thumb. One end of the thimble is fitted to hold either a thin piece of chalk or a slate pencil. The old stand-by of magicians—the flesh-colored thumb-tip—is a useful device for this purpose. The apparatus should be well made, not merely a crudely fashioned article.

In the original version, the magician produced the message on the slate by holding the slate in his hand with one side toward the spectators. His thumb, in back of the slate, secretly inscribed the message. This trick required adept work and it had certain limitations that rendered it inferior to other accepted methods.

Now, however, it appears in a new guise. The magician uses two slates, which are examined. They are placed on a table and each side is numbered with a piece of chalk—1, 2, 3, and 4. The slates are immediately placed together; a message appears between them. Each side, it must be noted, is turned toward the spectators during the numbering process.

Even magicians may wonder how the thumb-tip and its chalk enter into this slate-writing trick, for the method has been improved by the addition of a very clever form of manipulation.

HOW MESSAGE IS WRITTEN AND COVERED.

The performer writes the message on one slate as he carries the slates to the table. To do this effectively, he has the table set a considerable distance away. He holds the slates together with one surface toward the audience and writes with his thumb on the rearmost side. When he lays the slates on the table, he puts down the front slate first; then the back slate, with its writing side down. The writing should be near one end of the slate; and this end is toward the back of the table.

Reaching in his pocket for a piece of chalk, the wizard disposes of the thumb-tip. He picks up the uppermost slate, with his thumb on top and his fingers beneath. He writes the figure 1 on the upper surface. In turning up the other side of the slate he sees to it that his hand covers the message, the extended fingers doing this to perfection. He writes the figure 2 on that side and puts the slate on the table, turning it writing side down. There is no trickery in marking the other slate with numbers 3 and 4, but to be consistent, the magician holds the slate just as he held the first one. He puts the slates together, side 2 going on side 3. The slates are then ready for the appearance of the message.

This trick requires rather small slates. The message must be very short—say a number of four figures, or some initials. For the writing cannot cover much space, otherwise the fingers would not be able to conceal it.

SPIRIT SLATE EFFECT

This version of the spirit slate-writing trick is both simple and convincing. It requires very little skill, yet is well designed. The articles used are two slates and a pocket handkerchief. Both sides of both slates are shown clean; each is marked with an identifying letter or numeral. Yet when the slates are tied together and placed in the hands of the audience, a message appears on the inner surface of one slate.

Preparation is made beforehand. A short message—preferably a single word—is written across one slate, between the sides. A handkerchief is folded into a long strip. It is placed upon a table and the slate with the message is placed upon it. The message side of the slate is down and runs directly along the line of the kerchief.

The second slate is placed upon the first and the ends of the handkerchief are knotted above the upper slate. In this condition the broad center of the handkerchief conceals the message in the middle of the lower slate.

The magician brings on the slates. He carries a piece of chalk with one hand, holding the tied slates care-

lessly with the other. He speaks of psychic manifestations and his ability to reproduce them. Advancing, he
brings the slates upward and reveals the side that bears
the message. The word, of course, is hidden by the
broad center of the handkerchief.

The magician taps the surface of the slate with the
chalk and asks for a figure or a letter. This being given,

HOW HANDKERCHIEF COVERS MESSAGE ON SLATE.

he marks the corner of the slate accordingly, say with
the letter A. He turns the slates over and taps the opposite side. This he marks with a letter—B, for instance—
and sets the slates on the table, with the handkerchief
knot upward. He does this to untie the knot. He picks
up the upper slate in a careless manner, letting the
spectators observe the side marked B. Then he picks up
the lower slate, showing its clean, unmarked side. He
turns the upper slate so that the unmarked side is toward
the audience. He lays down the lower slate so that he
can mark the clean side of the upper slate with the
letter C. Laying down the upper slate, he lifts the lower
slate and marks its clean side D. At no phase of this
routine is the side that bears the letter A revealed.

He puts the A and D slate upon the other one, keeping the D side up. The message (on side A) is now
between the two slates. The slates are set upon the
center of the handkerchief, which is twisted slightly.
The ends of the handkerchief are knotted on top of the
slates. The slates are given to a spectator to hold. When
the handkerchief is untied, the message is found on the
side marked A.

While this routine requires no manipulation and involves no special apparatus, it must be performed in a decisive manner, with every possible effort to sell the idea to the audience. It is an excellent deception from a psychological standpoint. The very boldness with which side A is shown with the handkerchief in place serves to divert suspicion. Side B, it will be noted, is marked while the handkerchief is upon it; but the fact that the knot is untied and the surface of the slate is casually exhibited leads the spectators to forget that side A was not also shown in that manner.

The showing of the blank sides of both slates and the marking of each in turn are also effective. The placing of the upper slate upon the table before the lower brings the message within the slates in a subtle manner. The final touch is the narrowing of the handkerchief, before tying up the slates. When the handkerchief is taken off at the conclusion, its width is less than the height of the letters in the message. This completely eliminates any suspicion that might lurk in the minds of the observers.

This is a slate test of the highest efficiency and it will deceive all who look for complicated methods or who suspect some mechanical secret. The message used should be forced upon the audience in some manner. The name of a playing card . . . a word from a book . . . or the total of added numbers—these are all usable. The forcing is done while the slates are tied and in the possession of the expectant audience.

SINGLE-SLATE TRICK

This is a very useful spirit slate for close work. It is simply a single slate, which is shown blank on both sides. It is wrapped in newspaper or placed in a paper bag. When it is removed, it bears a message. The slate is given for inspection. The paper is crumpled and thrown away.

The slate has an improvised flap, which is merely a piece of black tissue paper or carbon paper. This covers a message that has been written on the slate. The paper flap is held in place by dabs of wax on the corners.

When the slate is wrapped in paper or put into a bag, the magician pushes the tissue paper so that it comes loose. Then the slate is withdrawn alone. The paper is crumpled and thrown away with the black paper inside it, taking away suspicion from the paper. The slate itself furnishes no clue to the mystery.

The very simplicity of this method makes it useful and eliminates many complications that are apt to arise when the flap slate is used at a small gathering.

NEWSPAPER TEST

This is a special test which may be shown on certain occasions. It is particularly good with a fair-sized group of people present. The magician sends some one to obtain the day's newspapers. He wants a copy of every local paper and may also call for a few out-of-town papers, as he can use any number up to ten.

The papers, when procured, are laid in a row on the table. They are numbered from left to right. The magician shows two slates and puts them together. He takes a pack of cards, shuffles it, and places it in a hinged wooden box. He states that the numbers on the top three cards will indicate: first, the newspaper; second, the page; third, the column. Face cards stand for eleven, twelve, and thirteen (jack, queen, and king).

The box is opened. The first card (say a three) enables the magician to select a newspaper. The next two cards (say eight and five) tell the page and column. The magician reads the headline of the chosen column. The slates are opened. On one slate appears the headline, written in chalk.

Old methods are used in this trick. The message is

written on a "spirit slate." It is covered with a flap. The wooden box is a "card box." It has a flap in the top portion. The flap hides three cards, which are arranged to indicate the desired numbers, say three, eight, and five. The magician picks the fifth column of the eighth page in one of the daily newspapers. He simply places this newspaper number three in the line.

From that point, the trick virtually works itself. The card box forces the three cards, the proper headline is discovered, and the message is revealed on the slate after the slates are separated.

The magician should explain that face cards mean to continue counting: for instance, eleven would be three columns over on the next page, as most newspapers have only eight columns. A face card indicating a newspaper in the row would mean counting to the end of the row and then continuing from the beginning. It is best to have a small card indicate the newspaper; then the magician is not dependent upon any particular number of newspapers. He is sure to have at least three or four. Others may be added to the row, according to the quantity that is procured.

Another plan is to have a pack with all cards above the eights removed. It is also wise to have more than three cards above the flap in the card box; otherwise the flap will show when the top three cards are removed. A few more cards in place will keep the flap concealed.

Part Five

MESSAGE-READING

Houdini made a careful study
of various methods employed in the
reading of sealed messages.
From those, the author has selected
the ones that are evidently designed
for performing magicians.
These are more effective than the
usual billet readings used by
fraudulent mediums, as they can be
shown before larger audiences.

Houdini's notes contain various references to methods used by crystal-gazers who answer questions written by the audience. This act is done by trickery. It gradually reached a point of widespread presentation, and in order that the reader may fully understand the act, it is necessary to give a brief résumé of the usual methods before discussing improvements noted by Houdini.

The performer allows spectators to write questions and to seal them in envelopes. These questions are brought on the stage and are burned. Then the performer gazes into a crystal ball and begins to give "impressions" of questions that have been written. His statements are accurate and he follows by giving answers to the questions.

There are gullible persons who believe that this exhibition shows genuine telepathic power on the part of the crystal-gazer, and it is a regrettable fact that some charlatans have taken advantage of that situation to prey upon the susceptibilities of their audiences. But from the magician's view, the crystal-gazing act is merely a form of trickery. To be presented legitimately, it should be simply a form of entertainment, in which the spectators are mystified by the performer's ability to state what they have written—not by his ability to give answers to the questions.

There are two essential elements in this act. First, the performer must secretly preserve some of the questions written by the audience. Second, the wording of those questions must come into the performer's possession.

The conventional crystal-gazer adopted two methods. His assistants collected the written questions in long-handled velvet bags. These were known as "changing bags," because they had a double lining which could be changed by a simple turn of the handle. With the aid of this device, questions were gathered; the interior of

MESSAGES DROPPED IN BURNER. SOME GO
THROUGH PEDESTAL TO ASSISTANT BENEATH STAGE.

the bag was changed to open the other compartment; and when the bag was apparently emptied, a mass of duplicate envelopes fell into the burner. These dummy envelopes had been previously placed in the hidden section of the bag.

The assistants carried the apparently empty bags from the stage. Off stage, they opened the original envelopes while the performer was burning the duplicates. They learned the questions in the envelopes; their next step was to transmit that information to the performer.

The usual crystal-gazer wore a Hindu costume, with a large turban. There was a purpose in the costume. His turban concealed earphones; wires passed down to his shoes, which had metal plates on the bottom. The stage was fitted with plates, connected by wires to a transmitter. By stepping on the plates, contact was formed, and the crystal-gazer could hear the voice of his off-stage assistant, telling him the contents of the envelopes.

This system was used by many performers. Despite its effectiveness, there was a constant effort to supply some improved method. The electrical system was expensive and needed considerable attention. It sometimes became dead during a performance. There was always the difficulty of misunderstanding information given by the man off stage. The last-named objection was counteracted by a double system; the performer carried a microphone beneath his costume and the concealed assistant could hear what was said on the stage. This enabled the performer and the assistant to carry on a veiled conversation between themselves. It did not, however, solve the problem of trouble with the electrical apparatus.

The various methods of doing away with the wires and the Oriental costume are too numerous to give in detail, especially as some of them are far inferior to the electrical system. The methods explained among Houdini's notes are given here as representative of improved methods. They do away with both the changing bag and the wires.

PERFORMER READING MESSAGE.
NOTE ASSISTANT'S WORK BENEATH STAGE.

There is no actual exchange of questions. The performer simply preserves some of the questions. That is sufficient, as no performer attempts to answer all of the questions submitted. Time would be too short.

The questions are gathered by assistants, who use network bags with which an exchange would be impossible. The envelopes are delivered to the performer, who drops them into a burner that is mounted on a pedestal. In back of the burner is an opening in the pedestal. This passes to the stage and there is an open trap beneath the pedestal.

In dropping the envelopes, the performer takes only a portion in his right hand. He drops this cluster into the burner, then another cluster of envelopes. He continues thus until all the envelopes have been dropped. With each action of the right hand, the performer inserts his second finger between the envelopes, dividing them into two groups—one in front of the second finger, the other

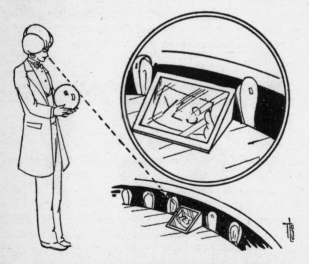

MAGNIFYING GLASS METHOD OF
SHOWING MESSAGES BETWEEN FOOTLIGHTS.

in back. He spreads the front group so that the envelopes there obscure those in back. As his hand approaches the burner, the rear group is behind the burner. When the envelopes are dropped, those in back drop behind the burner and go through the pedestal. This movement is perfectly natural and cannot be detected. Thus, from each cluster of envelopes the performer saves some, which are invisibly passed to the assistant under the stage. The questions in these envelopes are transmitted to the performer on the stage.

The first method of transmission is accomplished by means of another pedestal, upon which the crystal ball is set. Behind the pedestal is a slit in the stage. The assistants below stage write the questions in large letters on pieces of cardboard. One by one, these statements are pushed up behind the pedestal. Standing behind the pedestal, with the crystal in his hand, the performer sees each message as it comes into view.

The second method of transmission is even more ingenious. At the front of the stage, between the footlights, is an opening, covered with a lens of magnifying glass. Two of the footlights are turned to illuminate the glass, which can be seen only by the performer. The actual questions are placed against the glass. The performer sees them and has no difficulty in reading them, unless they are virtually illegible, in which case they are either rewritten by the assistants or are ignored.

Referring again to the obtaining of the questions, Houdini's notes give a method of actual exchange by the aid of the pedestal and burner. This is obviously intended for use with a small audience when the performer is desirous of answering most of the questions.

The pedestal has the opening which leads through the stage, but in this case there is a slide that covers the opening. At the back of the burner is a clip which contains a stack of dummy envelopes. The performer holds the envelopes in his right hand and approaches the pedestal, with his left side toward the audience. He reaches to pick up the burner. His right hand goes in back of the burner and drops the envelopes into the opening in the pedestal. The hand moves forward, drawing the slide shut, and with the same movement gathers up the dummy envelopes from the clip.

The left hand picks up the burner, the right hand assisting momentarily. Then the right drops the dummy envelopes into the burner. The supposed questions are ignited; the burner is set back on the pedestal.

These methods of performing the crystal act do away with the Hindu costume.

SEALED-MESSAGE READING

This routine involves old principles in the reading of sealed messages. It possesses certain points of effectiveness that make it a decided improvement over the well-known ideas.

The performer approaches a person with a stack of small envelopes. He passes one envelope to the person. There is a card inside the envelope. The performer holds the envelope while the person writes something on the card. The writer turns the card downward and slides it into the envelope which the performer is holding. The envelope and card are burned; the performer then states what was written.

A special envelope is used. The face of the envelope is cut away. This envelope is the bottom one of the stack. The flap side of each envelope is downward. The top envelope of the stack is ordinary. It contains a card. It is given to the person. The card is removed. The performer takes back the envelope and puts it on the stack. While the person is writing the performer casually turns his hand over. He holds out the stack and turns back the flap of the envelope that is now on top. The person inserts the card. It is the prepared envelope which receives the card; but the entire procedure is so natural that every one assumes that the envelope is the same as the one originally given to the person.

In going toward an ash tray or burner, the performer holds the special envelope with its flap toward the writer. This enables the performer to read the message through the open face of the envelope. The burning of the envelope and the card destroys all evidence of trickery.

For reading a series of questions, the performer can apply this principle to the old "one ahead" system, which is described herewith. All the envelopes are flaps upward. The prepared envelope is on top of the stack. The cards are separate from the envelopes. They are given out to the persons present.

After questions have been written, the performer goes to one person and says: "Put your card in the envelope like this and seal the envelope." He demonstrates by placing the card, writing downward, in the prepared envelope. He retains that envelope, after sealing it. He gives out the other envelopes and lets the spectators insert their cards. No one suspects that the first envelope is tricked.

Having gathered all the envelopes, the performer notes the message on the first card. He puts that envelope at the bottom of the stack. Holding the top envelope to his forehead, he calls out the question that is

INSERTION OF CARD IN OPEN-FACED ENVELOPE.

in the prepared envelope. The writer verifies the fact that the question was written. Every one supposes that it is in the envelope now held by the performer. He opens the envelope, looks at the card and states that he was correct.

In so doing, the performer notes the words on the card from the ordinary envelope. He lays that card aside, takes another envelope from the stack and names the question which he has just read. It is verified, and the envelope is opened for the performer to check. He continues thus, always reading the question one envelope ahead of the answer. The last envelope is the prepared one. The performer states the question that he read in the previous envelope. He gives back the cards and throws away the envelopes, the prepared one among them.

SEALED-ENVELOPE TEST

This is a method of discovering questions that have been written by individuals who seal their papers in envelopes and retain the envelopes. It is particularly good because nothing is used except paper, pencils, and envelopes.

The performer has a stack of envelopes. On top of the stack are several prepared envelopes. These envelopes are double. The face is cut from an envelope. It is inserted in an ordinary envelope. A sheet of carbon paper is placed between the two faces. The flaps are sealed together. This has the appearance of an ordinary envelope.

In each of the prepared envelopes the performer has a slip of paper. One envelope, however, has an extra slip of paper, for a purpose that will become evident. The prepared envelopes are faces up. The ordinary envelopes—which are greater in number than the prepared ones—are faces down. They contain no slips of paper. Armed with his stack of envelopes, the performer is ready.

He approaches his audience. He gives out the prepared envelops, drawing the slip of paper from each one. He lets the inside of each envelope be observed by the person who receives it. He puts the slip of paper on the envelope in each case and instructs the person to write and to hold the paper writing side down.

When this has been done, the performer remarks that he had an extra piece of paper in one envelope. He picks up the envelopes one by one, placing them upon the stack in his left hand until he obtains the one that has the extra slip of paper. He puts this envelope on the stack and places the stack under his left elbow. This enables him to use his hands in folding the blank piece of paper. He tells the spectators to fold their papers in that manner.

Bringing the stack of envelopes from his elbow, he naturally turns it over, and gives out the upper-most envelopes to the persons from whom he took envelopes. They naturally suppose that they are receiving the original envelopes. Instead, they are getting ordinary envelopes, while the performer is retaining the ones that have the carbon impressions.

Each person seals his paper in his envelope and retains the envelope. In case there are any additional persons from whom the performer did not take envelopes, a special procedure is adopted. The performer stops those persons while they are about to insert their papers. Dealing with each in turn, he takes the person's envelope and lays it on the stack in his left hand while he uses his right hand to show the blank piece of paper which he has folded. The person is careful to fold his paper properly enough to suit the performer. Then the performer gives him the envelope, but in so doing he turns the stack of envelopes so that an uprepared envelope is on top.

In brief, the performer, by subtle, natural procedure, exchanges for other envelopes the envelopes given out originally. There is nothing suspicious about this, as the writers do not know that the envelopes were prepared. They believe that they have written questions and have sealed them in ordinary envelopes, which are kept in their own possession.

Actually, the performer has the carbon impressions of the writing and can use them to reveal what the spectators have written. He can do this in several ways. He can open the envelopes secretly and learn the questions. He can pass the envelopes to an assistant who carries them off stage or from the room and later passes the information to the performer.

There are several simple and effective methods of doing this. The author is suggesting them here in order that the reader may utilize the principle of the prepared envelopes.

One method is for the assistant to write the questions in large letters on blank cards and to hold them so that the performer can see them, while they are invisible to the spectators. In this way, the first question is quickly sent to the performer, and while he is concentrating and answering it, the assistant prepares more large cards.

Another method is for the assistant to write the questions on a strip of paper and to bring the performer a crystal ball that rests upon a velvet-covered board. There is a shelf behind the board and the strip of paper rests upon it. The performer, in gazing at the crystal, learns the questions.

A new method, never before described, may be employed. In this system, the performer calls for some slates. The assistant does not appear immediately. He is transcribing the questions on the slates. The performer meanwhile tells the writers to concentrate. The slates are brought on with their blank sides toward the spectators. It is well to have one slate entirely blank. Holding the slates, the performer notes the writing on the rear slate. He lays down the slates and wipes both sides of the slate that is entirely blank. Then he writes an answer to one question on one side of the slate; and an answer to another question on the other side of the slate.

He picks up a second slate, but this time does not show both sides before he wipes the slate. He is noting the questions on the back of the slate as he cleans it. He cleans the front also, and writes the answer to a question on one side, the answer to a second question on the other side.

He continues thus with the remaining slates. Only three or four slates are necessary. This method leads up

DOUBLE ENVELOPE WITH HIDDEN CARBON PAPER.

to a very effective conclusion. The performer fails to answer one question. Perhaps he writes a wrong answer on a slate. He is determined to answer the question; and he does not care to rub out anything that he has written on the slates, because these writings are evidence of his answers to the questions.

So he calls for two more slates and the assistant appears with them. Both slates are shown blank; between them, the performer causes the correct answer to the last question to appear, apparently of its own accord. This is simply a spirit slate-writing trick, the methods of which are described in this book. The assistant has placed the correct answer on the spirit slates and the performer uses them.

A BILLET READING

Two persons work in this performance—the magician and another who is seated in a chair on the platform and who intends to reveal words that are secretly written by members of the audience.

The performer gives out small slips of paper, measuring about one by two inches. Words, numbers, or other notations are written on the slips. The performer then gathers them in a basket. The slips are numbered on the reversed sides or are of differently colored paper, so that each person can recognize his slip when it is to be returned to him.

Each slip is folded before it is placed in the basket. Nevertheless, the performer's assistant answers the question. The usual procedure is for the magician to have a lady assistant, who is blindfolded and seated with her back to the audience.

This ingenious performance depends upon the manner in which the magician secretly passes some of the slips to his female assistant. The transfer is accomplished despite the fact that the magician does everything to prove that such action is impossible.

The basket that he uses to collect the messages is small but deep. Its interior is covered with a dark, pleated cloth. There is a small secret pocket in the cloth at the side of the basket. This pocket contains a false thumb-tip made of metal. The tip will fit loosely on the magician's thumb and it is painted flesh-color.

When the magician hands out the slips, the basket is on the table with the thumb-tip in the secret pocket. The thumb-tip is mouth up. In collecting the slips, the magician allows them to be dropped into the basket; but with one person, he takes the slip himself and drops it. The magician lets it fall into the thumb-tip and with the same action he inserts his thumb into the metal

**TAKING TIP
FROM BASKET**

**REMOVING
TIP**

THE THUMB TIP CONTAINING MESSAGE IS
HELD BEHIND THE SLATE. THE MEDIUM REMOVES IT
WHEN SHE TAKES THE SLATE. HER BACK
IS TOWARD THE AUDIENCE.

device and brings it out of the pocket. He keeps his hand in motion as he carelessly shows it empty; hence the thumb-tip is not observed.

When all the slips are in the basket, it is replaced on the table at the front of the platform. The lady appears and seats herself in the chair with her back toward the audience. In arranging this position, the magician has ample opportunity to drop the thumb-tip into his assistant's lap. While he is preparing to blindfold the lady, she removes the slip from the thumb-tip, reads it and replaces it. The performer puts the bandage around her eyes and then picks up the thumb-tip from her lap.

The performer goes to the basket. He reaches in and inserts his thumb into the pocket, leaving the thumb-tip there; but he draws out the message which was in the thumb-tip. He also picks up another slip and drops it into the thumb-tip, which he brings out on his thumb. These actions take place while he is apparently choosing one folded slip which he wishes the lady to reveal. He gives the original slip to the person who wrote it— the slip being identified by its number or its color. It is obvious that the performer has had no opportunity to open the slip.

The performer now picks up a slate and carries it to the lady. She reaches above her head to receive it. The magician holds the slate vertically, with his thumb and its false tip out of view behind the slate. In taking the slate, the lady also carries away the thumb-tip.

She now lays the slate in her lap and writes the words that were on the original slip of paper, which is at present *held by the spectator*. She also has opportunity to read the second slip. The blindfold does not prevent her from seeing downward into her lap. She replaces the second slip in the thumb-tip. She holds up the slate with the writing away from the audience. Behind the slate she holds the thumb-tip in readiness for the performer. He takes the slate and inserts his thumb into the thumb-tip. He carries the slate to the spectators, who read the writing aloud and check it with the slip that the individual holds.

This is a very mystifying effect. The performer is ready to repeat it, for everything is set for a continuance of his procedure. He goes to the basket and obtains a third slip in his thumb-tip. He gives the second slip to the person who wrote it. He erases the writing on the slate and carries the slate to his female assistant.

The second slip is duplicated on the slate; the routine continues and a third message is written by the lady, then a fourth, and so on until the entire supply is exhausted. In giving the last slip to its owner, the performer merely removes it from the thumb-tip as he leaves the device in the secret pocket of the basket. He announces that he has reached the last slip and that the lady will answer it in conclusion. No more deception is necessary at that point.

This is a highly effective exhibition that will puzzle the shrewdest observers. There is very little chance of the thumb-tip's being detected. It is practically invisible when on the magician's thumb, especially as he can keep his thumb partially obscured from view except when his hands are in motion. The most important part of the demonstration is its smoothness. The entire routine requires careful rehearsal, and all hesitation or clumsiness should be avoided. It may be performed deliberately but pains should be taken to make it convincing throughout.

Part Six

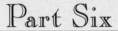

PLATFORM TRICKS

This section will appeal to all
who are interested in magic, as it
contains tricks designed for
presentation at close range or
before a large audience. It is a section
of small magic that includes
new ideas and improvements over
well-known tricks.

This is an entertaining routine with a silk handkerchief, which disappears and returns after the magician has completely misled his audience. It requires the following preparations:

(1) A red silk handkerchief under shirt collar at the right side of the neck.

(2) A green silk handkerchief under the left side of the shirt collar.

(3) A piece of red silk ribbon tucked under the right side of the vest.

(4) A metal finger-tip[1] which contains a corner of red silk.

(5) Two silk handkerchiefs on the table. One red, the other green.

The performer begins by showing the two handkerchiefs that are on the table. He asks the spectators to choose either color—red or green. It makes no difference which they choose; he uses the red. If they select red, he uses the red silk. If they call for green, he remarks that they have chosen green, which leaves him red. In either event, he calmly tucks the green silk into his coat pocket.

He rolls the red silk into a ball and places it in his left hand. He moves the right hand to the vest and pretends to push an imaginary silk out of sight. He draws out the end of the ribbon. The spectators see it and think it is a corner of the silk handkerchief. The magician observes their glances. He pulls the red ribbon from beneath his vest and looks at it in surprise. Then he opens his left hand to show that the red handkerchief is really there. This turns the laugh on the audience.

Again the magician rolls the red silk into a ball; this

---

[1] The finger-tip is similar to the thumb-tip, mentioned in this book. It is painted flesh-color and is hardly visible when on the tip of the finger, especially when the hand is kept in motion.

time he pretends to hold it in his left hand but actually palms it in the right. His hand goes to his vest as before and he boldly pushes the silk unseen beneath the vest, remarking: "It would be too apparent to try to place a handkerchief under my vest." He draws the hand away, leaving the silk, and continues to the trousers pocket, saying: "I would not attempt to hide it in the pocket, either."

This movement enables him to insert his forefinger in the finger-tip. He brings out the right hand and pokes the forefinger into the left fist, leaving the finger-tip. Then he draws the red silk corner into view, remarking: "With such keen observers watching me, it would be impossible to take the handkerchief unseen from the left hand."

He pokes the silk corner back into the finger-tip. He removes the right hand, with the tip on the finger, keeping the hand in motion. He points to the left again and opens the left hand. The red silk has vanished. The right hand goes to the collar. The finger-tip is left beneath the collar while the duplicate red silk is drawn into view.

While the audience is still wondering at the deception, the magician adds: "If you had selected green, the result would have been the same. Here is the green handkerchief, waiting under my collar." The left hand draws the duplicate green silk from its hiding-place and the performer makes his bow holding the red handkerchief in one hand and the green handkerchief in the other, just as when he began the trick.

THE VANISHING GLASS

Houdini's notes attribute this trick to De Kolta. A small glass is partly filled with water. It is placed in a cylinder of paper. The sheet of paper is crushed. The glass is gone.

The paper cylinder contains a metal ring which has two projecting clips, painted flesh-color. The ring is in place at the beginning of the trick. Its projecting clips extend through a slit in the side of the cylinder. This is kept to the rear.

The glass tapers slightly. It is set in the paper cylinder. Its bottom fits in the metal ring. The magician turns the cylinder (in his left hand) so that the slit is toward the audience. At the same time his right hand starts to smooth the paper; the projecting clips are gripped between the fingers. When the back of the right hand is toward the audience, the hand moves straight upward. The ring carries the glass, safely hidden in the palm of the right hand.

Meanwhile the left hand twists the cylinder so that the slit is not viewed by the audience. The left arm is raised as the right hand goes to the breast pocket of the coat. The pocket is held open by a strip of bent whale-

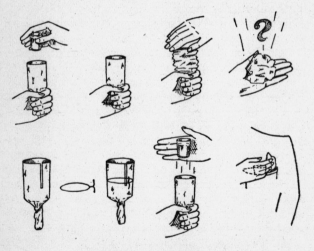

ROUTINE OF VANISHING GLASS.
NOTE SLIT IN PAPER—ALSO WIRE RING WHICH IS
CLIPPED BY FINGERS. THE GLASS
IS DROPPED IN THE POCKET.

bone. A handkerchief projects from in front. The right hand drops the glass into the pocket. It fits rather tightly and the water does not spill. The pocket should be lined with rubber in case of emergency.

The right hand then comes forward and the empty paper cylinder is crushed between the hands. The glass has unmistakably vanished and the paper may be torn to bits to conclude the trick.

This is an effect with good possibilities if performed smoothly and naturally. The removal of the glass is an excellent idea. The passage of the right hand to the pocket is covered by the left arm and the magician can create the impression that he is reaching for his handkerchief, which he finally decides not to use. If the glass is "stolen" neatly from the cylinder, there will be no suspicion on the part of the audience.

The illustrations show the effect and also give the details of the apparatus and the method by which the glass is secretly removed from the cylinder with the aid of the unseen wire ring.

A CLINGING WAND

(WITH THE WAND VANISH)

This is intended as an additional effect in conjunction with the "vanishing wand" used by many magicians. The wand in question is made of rolled paper, which is painted black on the outside. The nickeled metal tips of the wand are genuine; they are made of wood covered with metal tubing and they have short projections which fit tightly into the rolled black paper. Thus the wand is simply a hollow paper tube with solid ends.

The magician displays the wand as a solid one. He can drop the wand upon the floor or rap the ends against the table in the course of his performance. It passes as a wooden wand. When he is ready for the vanish, he

wraps the wand in a sheet of paper; then proceeds to
tear the paper to fragments. It is torn in half a dozen
pieces, which are tossed carelessly upon the floor to
prove that the wand has vanished. Only the end pieces
must be handled carefully, for these contain the metal
tips. They are reclaimed afterward and the tips are
fitted into another black paper tube to form another
wand suitable for disappearance.

There is another effect in which a wand clings to the
magician's fingers. These notes of Houdini's show how
the clinging effect may be adapted to the vanishing
wand. The wand is prepared beforehand by pushing
two black pins through it about three inches apart. The
points of the pins are dulled. The pins lie parallel
through the wand. They are invisible when the wand is
held, as it is kept so that the pin points are out of view.
Before wrapping the wand in paper, the magician places
his fingers upon the center of the wand and turns the
wand so that the pins are perpendicular to the fingers.
One pin is at one side of the hand; the other pin is at
the opposite side.

By simply spreading his fingers, the performer exerts
pressure against the extended pins. The wand then
clings to his hand in a most mysterious fashion. This
can be performed at fairly close range. While one hand
supports the wand in air, the other picks up the paper;
the wand is wrapped and immediately disappears.

The paper wand is admirably adapted to this trick, as
it is formed of tightly rolled layers of paper and the pins
are held firmly in place. The lightness of the wand also
makes it possible for the performer to turn the hand
about and move it in all directions without danger of
the wand's slipping.

The usual aftereffect of the wand trick is the repro-
duction of a solid wand which is made of wood with
nickeled tips. This is taken from the pocket, as though
it had passed there in some mysterious manner.

When performed as an opening trick, the solid wand
may be carried in the left sleeve. To produce it after the

vanish, the magician places a small pocketbook in his left hand, opens the purse, and extracts the wand with his right hand. The pocketbook is bottomless. Reaching through the opening with his fingers, the magician grips the end of the wand and pulls it through the pocketbook into the view of the audience. The back of the left hand and the left arm are turned toward the spectators during this production.

A VANISHING WAND

A wand is tapped against a table or another wand to prove that it is made of wood. It is dropped into an envelope. The envelope is crushed and torn to tiny pieces. Nothing remains of the wand.

The old familiar paper wand is used in this trick but with a new arrangement. The wand is made of black paper with silver paper tips; inside it there is a round piece of wood considerably shorter than the wand. This wood makes a noise when the wand is struck against the table.

The rounded wood is attached to a piece of cord elastic which runs up the magician's sleeve or beneath his coat; the elastic is stretched, but the wood is held within the wand by pressure of the hand.

When the magician picks up the long envelope, he releases the piece of wood and it leaves the wand. Only the paper wand goes in the envelope, and this can be completely destroyed. The notes suggest two wands for this trick, one in each hand. The magician first strikes the wands together, then vanishes them. This would be an excellent effect, but one somewhat more difficult than the trick with the single wand.

THE TRAVELING DIE

This trick requires a plate, a hat, a red silk handkerchief, and a large die. These are the principal properties seen by the audience. The die is shown to be solid. Attention is called to its large size—it almost fills the interior of the borrowed hat. The die is placed upon the plate. It is covered with a sheet of paper, which is pressed around it and twisted at the top.

The magician exhibits the silk handkerchief and rolls it between his hands. The handkerchief disappears. The paper is lifted from the plate. The handkerchief is found there; it has replaced the die. The hat is turned over and the solid cube of wood falls to the floor.

A reference to the accompanying illustrations will show the effect of this trick and also the principal points that form the explanation. The construction of the die has a great deal to do with the trick. The die is covered with a thin shell, which is open at the bottom. The shell is white on the inside, to resemble the paper that will later cover it. A duplicate silk handkerchief is pressed between the top of the real die and the inside of the shell. It is held in place by a rubber band, which can be instantly released by removing a blackened bit of match stick that holds one end of the loop.

It is a simple matter to demonstrate that the die is solid, by tapping the bottom of the genuine die. In showing that the die almost fills the interior of the hat, the magician dips his hand and releases pressure on the thin shell. The genuine die drops into the hat. Only the shell is retained by the performer.

The shell is placed upon the plate and the paper is molded about it. This action gives the magician the opportunity to release the rubber band so that the silk handkerchief fills the interior of the shell die. Now the magician vanishes the handkerchief. This may be done

in various ways. The most suitable is with the aid of a
"pull"—a cup-shaped metal container which is beneath
the coat, fastened to the end of a length of cord elastic.
The magician obtains the pull, works the handkerchief
into it, and releases the cup. The silk and its container
fly beneath his coat. The hands are shown empty.

When the paper cover is lifted, there is no trace of
the die. The shell is picked up with the paper and the
space formerly occupied by the die is now taken by
the silk handkerchief. The solid die is in the hat and the
magician concludes the trick by tilting the hat and letting the cube drop to the floor.

If desired, the shell die may be made of light cardboard; this will permit the magician to crumple the
paper after lifting it from the plate. This adds to the

THE SILK REPLACES THE DIE
BENEATH THE PAPER. THE SOLID BLOCK IS DISCOVERED
IN THE HAT. EXPLANATORY DIAGRAMS SHOW
HOW DUPLICATE SILK IS KEPT BETWEEN DIE AND SHELL;
ALSO HOW DIE IS LEFT IN HAT AND SHELL REMOVED.

effectiveness of the trick; it also means the destruction of the shell each time the trick is performed. The cost of the shell die is a trifling matter, however, if the magician finds that the apparent destruction of the paper makes the deception more convincing.

WITH THE LINKING RINGS

In performing the well-known Chinese ring trick, magicians have long desired a method whereby two rings could be unlinked and given for immediate examination. Here is a way of accomplishing it. Two ordinary

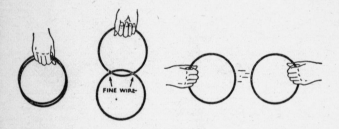

FINE WIRE

rings are used. Before the performance, they are tied together by two thin, silver-colored strings, so that they appear to be attached.

The magician can pick these up as if they were separate rings; then turn one ring downward so that the rings appear to join. The upper ring is held with the lower dangling beneath it. Apparently one ring is linked to the other, as the silver threads are virtually invisible while the rings sway back and forth.

By taking one ring in each hand and moving them back and forth, the magician easily breaks the strings, which drop unnoticed to the floor. The result is two single solid rings which can be immediately given for thorough inspection.

The threads should be tied tightly, a few inches apart, the space being arranged in accordance with the diameter of the rings. The purpose is to create an illusion of two rings actually joined and this is by no means difficult to do, especially as the magician is performing the usual ring routine.

A NEAT PRODUCTION TUBE

This tube is designed for the production of silk handkerchiefs, flags, ribbons, and other articles. The tube is shown empty and is set on a tray. Then the articles are produced.

It is simply an adaptation of an old principle. There are two tubes; the inner one is smaller than the outer. The inner tube is loaded with the various articles that are to be produced. It stands upon a chair, against the back. The tray is on the chair, leaning against the back, its upper edge above the tube.

After showing the outer tube empty—to the audience, this is the only tube—the magician reaches for the tray with his left hand. He swings the upper edge of the tray forward before he lifts it and his right hand simply sets the large tube over the smaller one. The magician holds the tray with both hands, striking it to prove it is solid. Then he places it upon a table and sets the tube upon it, lifting both tubes as one. He is ready to produce the various articles from the tube. The outer tube should be made of cardboard or very thin metal, so that the inner tube can be gripped by squeezing the outer.

The author has added a great improvement to this trick, without altering the routine. The addition also simplifies the working, as will be seen from the following description:

NOTE HOW BOTTLE IS "LOADED" IN TUBE
WHEN LIFTING TRAY. SILKS ARE PRODUCED;
THEN GLASS AND BOTTLE.

Instead of using a simple inner tube, the performer has a metal bottle of a type used in several magical effects. This bottle is hollow and bottomless. Just below the neck is a horizontal partition that forms the bottom of a compartment which contains liquid. The bottle is about the size of a quart bottle; it is painted black and bears a label. The compartment is filled with liquid, and the bottle is corked.

A glass is placed in the bottom of the trick bottle. The glass is bottom upward and the rest of the space is packed so tightly with silk handkerchiefs and flags that the whole load is kept in place. This bottle simply takes the place of the customary inner tube. It is covered by the outer tube, which has been shown empty. The bottle is much easier to cover than the ordinary inner tube because of its neck and tapering shoulders. The cardboard tube can be virtually dropped upon it.

When the magician places the tube upon the tray, he inverts the tube and thus gets at the handkerchiefs and flags. Having produced them, he lifts the tube and tilts it toward himself. He shows surprise, and reaching in, brings out the glass. This gives him the opportunity to invert the tube again, in a very natural manner.

He still holds the glass in his hand. He peers into the tube, then lifts it with his free hand and reveals the bottle. He sets down the glass, draws the cork from the bottle, and pours out a glassful of liquid.

This makes an excellent conclusion to the trick, as the bottle appears to be quite ordinary and the production of so solid an object makes the previous production of silks even more mysterious. Inasmuch as the inner tube is a necessary evil, its production in the form of a bottle is in this case turned to the magician's advantage.

PERFECTION PAPER-TEARING

This is a variation of the paper-tearing trick in which a strip of tissue paper is destroyed and is later reproduced whole. In the usual method, the trick is performed with the aid of a false thumb-tip made of metal. The magician shows his hands empty and proceeds to tear the strip of tissue paper. As he gathers the torn pieces, he draws the thumb-tip from his right thumb and retains it in the left hand. At this point he brings his right thumb noticeably into view. While the thumb actually wears the false tip, it is not made conspicuous.

In wadding the torn strips, a duplicate, folded strip is brought from the thumb-tip and the torn pieces are put there instead. Then the right thumb regains the thumb-tip. When the tissue paper is unfolded, it is apparently restored and the hands are shown empty.

The trick in this form has been long used by magicians ever since the time when the celebrated Chinese wizard, Ching Ling Foo, brought it into popularity. Much depends upon the presentation, as a capable performer can make the trick appear almost miraculous.

The improvement in the present method lies in the use of three strips of paper instead of one. These strips are of different colors: black, orange, and green. In the thumb-tip is a strip formed into a circle; black, orange, and green pasted together. There are also three cards: black, orange, and green, respectively. The thumb-tip is concealed beneath the three strips of loose paper, which lie on the tray. Each strip is approximately two feet long. The individual portions of the circle in the thumb-tip are of corresponding length.

The magician advances with the tray and asks some person to take the cards. The magician picks up the three strips of paper; in doing so, he obtains the thumb-tip with his right thumb. He lays the tray aside and proceeds to tear the three strips. He asks the spectator to decide in what order he desires the restored strips to appear: black, green, orange; orange, black, green; or any possible combination. The spectator names his choice, showing the three cards in order. The performer restores the torn papers so that they form a long single strip corresponding to the spectator's choice.

The secret is very simple. It has been mentioned that the duplicate strip is a circle formed by three strips. It is possible to form any combination of the three colors by simply tearing the circle at the proper join. For instance; if orange, green, and black is required, the circle is broken between orange and black; if green, orange, and black is desired, the circle is broken between green and black. The combination runs from left to right or from right to left according to the manner in which the performer exhibits the restored strip.

The simplest rule is to remember the color first named and the color last named and to break the paper where those two colors join, then retain the end of the color first named, letting the strip hang downward. The free hand may point out the three colors from top to bottom, showing that they have met the requirements imposed by the selector.

CONE AND EGG

Houdini enjoyed performing old tricks that were classics in magic and which had been almost forgotten in the modern era of conjuring. His notes contain many references to tricks of this sort. In the material was the following routine with the old cone and orange. It is probably intended for a small-sized cone, as an egg is used instead of an orange.

The cone is a wooden article. It is actually a truncated cone with a special rounded top. The magician borrows a hat and places it on a side table. He exhibits the wooden cone and wraps a piece of paper about it, fastening the paper with pins. He sets a large plate on the hat and puts an egg on the plate. He lifts the paper cover from the cone and sets the paper cover on the egg.

He raps the solid cone with his wand and covers it with a handkerchief. He walks forward and tosses the cloth in the air. The cone has vanished. The magician lifts the paper cover and reveals the cone upon the plate. A moment later he produces the egg from his elbow.

He replaces the cover over the cone. He makes several passes with the egg and finally squeezes it between his hands. The egg disappears completely. The cover is lifted to reveal the egg upon the plate. The magician sets the plate aside and places the cover with it. He tilts the hat and shows the cone inside. He concludes by breaking the egg, crumpling the paper, and returning the hat to its owner, at the same time bringing the wooden cone for examination.

There are actually two solid cones used in this trick; also a thin metal shell that fits over a cone and is painted to resemble it. At the outset, one cone is on a servante (hidden shelf) behind the side table. The magician borrows the hat and uses it for some byplay, finally taking it to the table, where he secretly "loads" the cone into the hat. It remains there awaiting the finish of the trick.

Next the magician exhibits the second cone—the first seen by the audience—which is already covered with the thin metal shell. He forms a paper cover, using the cone as a mold and when he raises the cover, he carries the metal shell along inside it. He sets a plate upon the

THE DRAWINGS SHOW VARIOUS PHASES
OF THE TRICK AND GIVE A "BACK STAGE" VIEW
OF THE IMPORTANT MANOEUVRES.

hat and puts an egg on the plate. He covers the egg with a supposedly empty paper cover.

He vanishes the solid cone by covering it with a handkerchief of double thickness. Between its layers, the cloth has a pasteboard disk. The magician inverts the cone as he places the cloth over it. He is standing behind his center table at the time and he lets the cone drop to a servante at the rear of that table. The cardboard disk retains the shape of the bottom of the cone. The spectators believe that the cone is still in the large handkerchief. The cone seems to vanish when the magician tosses the handkerchief in the air.

While the cloth is still falling, the magician turns toward the side table. As he steps in that direction, he obtains a duplicate egg from beneath his vest. He lifts the paper cover, leaving the metal shell cone. The vanished cone has apparently replaced the egg. The magician produces the duplicate egg at his elbow. He puts the paper cover back over the shell cone.

Now comes the byplay—false passes with the egg. In one maneuver, the magician pretends to carry the egg beneath his coat with his left hand. He suddenly shows the egg in the right hand and smiles at the suspicious glances of the spectators. This false movement to the coat enables the magician to obtain a special "pull" —a spring-wire holder attached to a length of cord elastic that passes beneath the coat. The egg is wedged into the pull. It flies beneath the coat under the cover of the arm. The hands are shown empty.

The magician approaches the side table and lifts the paper cover. He carries the shell cone with it. The egg has returned. Lowering the cover behind the hat, the magician releases the metal shell. It falls into the servante behind the table. The cover is laid on the center table with the egg and the plate. The solid cone is produced from the hat.

Having disposed of the shell, the magician can now crush or otherwise destroy the paper cover. He breaks the egg to show that it is genuine and when he returns the hat to the audience, he carries with him the only remaining article—one solid wooden cone.

HOUDINI'S AFGHAN BANDS

Among Houdini's notes on magic is a finale for the Afghan band trick. It appears without diagrams; hence the details of working it must be left in some degree to the individual performer. The instructions given here are more specific than Houdini's actual notes; but the author has adhered quite closely to the original rather than depart from the idea itself. The trick has all the elements of practicability but requires actual experiment in order to determine the best method of presentation. It should prove of unusual interest to readers of magic, as there have been more experiments with the Afghan bands than with almost any other trick in small magic.

The original Afghan band trick was performed with three circular strips of paper. The ends of the strips were glued to form the circle. One band was cut in half and it quite naturally formed two separate circles. The second band was cut. Like the first, it formed two loops, but they were linked together—a most surprising result. The third band was cut. The result was even more remarkable. The band came out in one large, narrow circle, double the size of the original.

The Afghan bands were highly recommended, but seldom used, chiefly because the cutting of the paper was a tedious process. Some years ago, magicians began to perform the trick with circles of muslin instead of paper. By having a slit in the center of each muslin loop, it became a question of ripping instead of cutting and the trick was worth while. Credit for first using bands of muslin has been given to Carl Brema, the well-known magical dealer.

The strange behavior of the bands is due to their formation. To make a band form two separate loops, simply place the ends together and glue them. To make a band form two linked loops, give one end a double twist before gluing. To make a band form a large circle twice the size of the first, give one end a single twist before gluing. It may be noted that with paper, it is difficult to conceal the twists. This is not so with muslin, which can be pressed flat.

The modernized version of the Afghan bands came about through experiments made by James C. Wobensmith, past president of the Society of American Magicians. He applied the principle to one wide band. The band is first split a few inches at the center of one end, before gluing. One half of the split end is given a single twist; the other half is given a double twist. Then the ends are glued. The result: the band, when torn in half, forms two separate bands. When one of these narrow bands is torn, it forms two bands linked together. When the other narrow band is torn, it forms a band of twice the size. Muslin is used as the material. The trick is highly effective.

Houdini used this trick in his matinée performances, and he refers to it in connection with the finale that he devised. The finale is performed with three bands of muslin: red, white, and blue, each separate.

These three bands may first be used to produce the old effects; if this proves too complicated, the performer can have a number of bands available and pick up three fresh bands for the finale. The author recommends this latter course. The three single bands are looped one within the other, the blue band being on the outside. The magician tears the bands in half. He drops one portion and reveals the other. The result is a triple link, formed by red, white, and blue bands.

The secret lies in the use of two extra bands—one red, the other white—and a double blue band. In preparing, the red is linked into the white; and the white is linked into the blue, which is double width. The blue band is folded in half and the red and white bands are pressed inside the fold, which is stitched along the open edge. This bears the appearance of a single blue band and it is laid folded on a table, care being taken to cover the spot where the link of the white band shows through.

In presenting, the performer picks up an ordinary red band and an ordinary white band and places them with the prepared blue band. The magician pretends to tear the three bands. In reality, he merely rips open the double blue band, the sound of the tearing creating the required illusion. At the finish, the single bands are tossed aside and three linked bands are exhibited. Apparently three of the bands have not joined, while the other three have formed a chain.

Houdini suggests a further finale to the trick—a very large band concealed beneath the top of the vest. This band could be a single color, or it could be composed of three colors—red, white, and blue. The lower part of the band is weighted. Attached to the upper part of the band is a fine loop of thread or catgut, which extends from the vest. The band is rolled or pleated within the vest.

Finishing his triple link effect, the magician gathers in the colored bands so that they form a bundle. His hands come close to his body and his right thumb engages the loop that extends from the vest. The hands move quickly upward and outward. The large band follows and appears instantly as it begins to unroll. The magician drops the smaller bands and whirls the huge band around his forefinger, the weight at the bottom of the loop aiding him in this maneuver. The effect is that the large band has been conjured from nowhere and its appearance, as it whirls above the magician's head, marks an effective conclusion to the routine with the Afghan bands.

THE VANISHING TABLE LEG

This is an elaboration of the "Vanishing Wand" trick. It concerns the vanish and reappearance of the nickel-plated rod which forms the center leg of a typical table used by a magician.

The table consists of three parts; a tripod base, the center rod and the top. It is taken to pieces. The top and the base are laid aside. The center rod is rapped to prove its solidity—the fact that it supported the top being silent proof of the same fact—and it is wrapped in a sheet of paper. The paper is crumpled. The rod has vanished. Taking a silk hat, the magician draws forth the missing table leg.

The center rod used on the table has an outer shell of glazed silver paper. This does not detract from its appearance of solidity. It is necessary to dispose of the

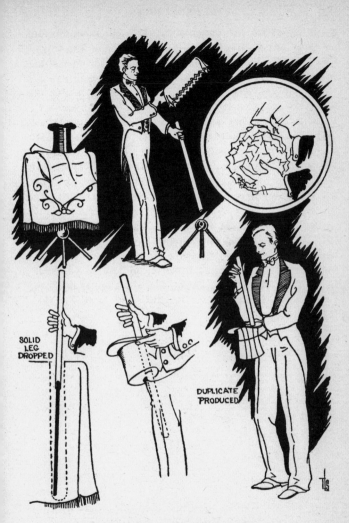

TABLE TRICK. SOLID LEG VANISHES
WHEN WRAPPED IN PAPER. THE LOWER DRAWINGS
SHOW HOW SOLID LEG LEAVES
PAPER SHELL; ALSO THE PRODUCTION OF
THE DUPLICATE TABLE LEG.

solid leg within the paper shell. This is accomplished with the aid of another table at the side of the stage. The side table has a long drape and a well in the tabletop. A long bag extends downward from the well.

On the side table is a sheet of newspaper; upon this a hat. The magician carries the rod in his right hand. In order to lift the hat and remove the sheet of paper, he finds it necessary to use both hands. Holding the end of the rod behind the hat, he lets the solid rod drop into the well, his hand retaining the paper shell. This shell is wrapped in the newspaper. Inasmuch as the rod never leaves the sight of the spectators, the ruse is not suspected.

The newspaper is crumpled, destroying the paper shell. The metal rod has apparently vanished. Beneath his vest and in the right side of his trousers leg, the magician has a duplicate table leg. There is a hole in the bottom of the hat. By holding the hat against his vest, the magician brings out the solid table leg that matches the original.

Part Seven

STAGE TRICKS

These are large tricks,
suited to the professional magician.
Some of them were planned
or obtained by Houdini for use in
his own stage performances.
They comprise a varied array of
large and effective magic.

THE TRAVELING BALL

This is a stage trick that requires two cubical boxes, each set upon a metal rod. Each box has a solid bottom and a solid top. The four sides drop downward.

The magician takes a large, heavy ball and places it in the box at the right. He closes the doors of the box. He also closes the box at the left. He then commands the ball to pass from the box at the right to the box at the left. When the boxes are opened, the ball has obeyed the order. It is in the box at the left. The box at the right is empty.

The trick depends upon the use of two rubber balls —thick toy balloons. The balloon used in the box at the right has a special valve which allows an even discharge of air when released. This ball is placed in its box. The rear door is the last one closed. The valve is at the rear. The performer opens the valve just before he closes the door. To aid the disappearance of the ball, the box has a double top. A flat board descends upon the sinking ball and presses the deflated balloon flat, so that it is finally lost between a double bottom. This special top is released by a catch at the back of the box and it is arranged to move downward evenly.

The box at the left also contains a balloon, which is deflated at the outset. The sliding board is not essential to this box, as the balloon can be carefully pressed in the bottom of the box. It can be covered by a thin false bottom if desired, for the false bottom will rise to the top of the cabinet when the balloon expands. The valve is beneath the balloon and a hose is attached. The hose runs through the rod that supports the box. As soon as the box is closed, air is forced through the hose and the balloon is inflated.

The main details of the trick are shown in the explanatory diagram. The hose can come up through the stage, or it can run behind the scenes under a carpet. A

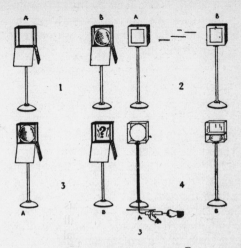

1, BALL SHOWN IN STAND B.
2, STANDS CLOSED. 3, BALL ARRIVES IN
A. 4, WORKING DETAILS OF APPARATUS.

hand pump may be used for the inflation, or a small container of compressed air may be utilized. The assistant who handles this should know the approximate amount of air required.

The bottoms of the boxes are slightly lower inside than outside, as this aids in the concealment of the balls. Each ball should be colored to represent a granite ball or a cannon ball, whichever the performer chooses to use.

Just before the trick, the performer introduces a ball that is actually solid. He exchanges this for the rubber ball that goes into the first box. There are several methods of effecting an exchange. Perhaps the best is to drop the solid ball near the side of the stage. It rolls off and is overtaken by an assistant who brings back the rubber ball, carrying it as though it were very heavy.

Houdini suggests an exchange by means of a trap in the stage, first covering the ball with a cloth and then disclosing it after placing it in the box. This method is hardly suitable, as the special preparation of a trap would be a great deal of unnecessary trouble for anything less than an illusion.

KELLAR'S WINE AND RIBBON

On a table in the center of the stage stands a large bottle. The magician picks up the bottle and pours out glasses full of wine. These are served to the audience. The magician points to the bottle. A piece of ribbon emerges from the neck. The magician draws the end of the ribbon. He continues to pull, bringing many yards of white ribbon from the bottle. While he is drawing the ribbon, he calls for a color. Suppose that green is named. When the white ribbon is exhausted, the magician walks away. The end of a green ribbon suddenly appears from the neck of the bottle. The green ribbon is drawn forth. The same effect is repeated with other colors.

The magician asks for the names of various countries. One by one the flags of those countries bob up and each flag is taken from the bottle and displayed. At the conclusion, another flag appears without being called for. The magician shows it and places it upon the bottle. At his command, the flag suddenly disappears back into the bottle.

Finally, the magician asks a volunteer to aid him. Many more yards of ribbon are extracted from the bottle and at the conclusion of the trick the bottle is broken with a hammer to prove that it is quite ordinary.

Two bottles are used. The first is made of metal. It has a cavity running right through the center. The diagrams show its construction. Wine is contained around the sides of the bottle. The bottle rests upon a table which has a hollow top and a hollow leg. The white ribbon runs up through the leg and in the top of the table. A thread passes from the ribbon, through the bottle and out to the stage. The thread is loose. Hence the magician can use the bottle to pour out wine.

When the serving is finished, the bottle is stood upon the table. The thread is drawn tight, either by the magician or by a concealed assistant. The final tightening of the thread causes the end of the white ribbon to put in its appearance. While the white ribbon is coming out, another color is demanded. An assistant below stage fastens the required ribbon on the end of a thread which is attached to the lower end of the white ribbon. After all the white ribbon has been produced, the magician gathers it up. As he steps away from the table, the thread draws the next ribbon into view.

This continues with all the ribbons. During the production of the last ribbon, the magician stops and calls for the names of countries. The assistant below hears his replies and arranges the various flags in their proper order, each connected to the one above by a length of thread. Stepping away with the last ribbon, the magi-

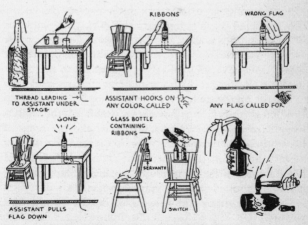

DETAILS OF WINE AND RIBBON TRICK.

cian causes the first flag to appear. Each flag is produced in succession by the same method. The final flag
is one that is not wanted. The magician removes it
almost entirely from the bottle; in so doing he breaks
the thread that connects it with the flag previously
produced. Deciding that he does not want the flag, he
drapes it over the top of the bottle and commands it to
disappear.

A strong cord is attached to the lower corner of the
flag—the corner which is never removed from the bottle. The assistant pulls the cord when he hears the
magician's command. The flag is drawn down through
the bottle and into the table. The magician corks the
bottle. He carries it to a chair upon which he has placed
the ribbons. On the back of the chair is a servante—a
bag large enough to hold the bottle. A duplicate glass
bottle is also resting behind the chair. Under cover of
the flags and ribbons, the magician has ample opportunity to drop the metal bottle secretly and bring out
the glass bottle in its stead.

The glass bottle is packed with ribbons of various
colors. They are fastened together, having been previously pushed into place with the aid of a wand. The
ribbons are hidden by the cork in the neck of the bottle.
The magician simply removes the cork and, with the
aid of a volunteer assistant, produces quantities of silk
ribbon. As a quart bottle will hold yards and yards of
ribbon, this is very effective, as it appears to be a con-
tinuation of the productions that took place while the
bottle was on the table.

When all the ribbons have been produced, the trick is
brought to an effective conclusion by the breaking of
the bottle. This convinces the audience that a real
mystery has been performed. An ordinary glass bottle
that has held a large supply of wine and innumerable
yards of ribbon is indeed a marvelous article.

The illustrations show various details of the apparatus.

HAT SUSPENSION

The magician appears wearing evening clothes. He stands at the back of the stage, between two draped curtains. He removes his hat and bows to the audience. He places his hat upon his head and then slowly stoops forward. The hat remains suspended in the air. The magician looks up at the hat. He steps behind it and makes passes with his hands. The hat slowly descends. It rises at command. It reaches the level of the magician's hand. He plucks it from the air, twirls it between his fingers and walks forward to make another bow to the audience.

THE FLOATING HAT—WITH SPECIAL VIEW
OF ASSISTANTS CONCEALED AT SIDES OF ARCHWAY.

This is a good opening trick. It depends upon two assistants who are standing well behind the curtains. Each assistant is mounted on a footstool. Threads pass from one assistant to the other. There are two threads, the ends being hooked to the shoulders of the assistants.

When the magician appears, he bows while he is behind the threads. He removes his hat as he does so. In concluding his bow, he stands up beneath the threads and his head presses against the threads. He places his hat upon his head. The hat actually rests upon the threads, due to its broad brim. The threads are taut and when the magician stoops, the hat remains upon the threads above him. He looks upward in surprise and moves backward. From that position he commands the hat to descend and to rise. The assistants step down slowly from the stools, taking care to control the hat by correct handling of the threads. By lowering and raising their bodies, they can cause the hat to go up or down, but it never reaches its original height. It is finally taken by the magician. While he twirls it, the assistants detach the threads from their shoulders. The threads fall upon the stage. The magician is free to walk forward without disturbing the threads.

This is a good opening trick. It requires coöperation on the part of the assistants to make it successful. Properly done, it should prove a real mystery. According to Houdini's notes, this trick was shown by Ching Ling Foo, at a special performance in a club in New York.

A NEW DYEING TUBE

This device will be of special interest to magicians, as it is an improvement over the old tubes used for changing the colors of silk handkerchiefs. In order to make the idea plain to the reader, we must first briefly consider the effect of the usual "dye tube." The magician rolls a sheet of paper and pushes white silk handkerchiefs through it. One silk comes out red, another white, the third blue. These three are then pushed through the tube. They are transformed into a large American flag.

The tube seen by the audience is simply made of paper or cardboard, but there is also an inner tube, which may be termed the "fake tube." The fake holds the other handkerchiefs and the flag. When the different

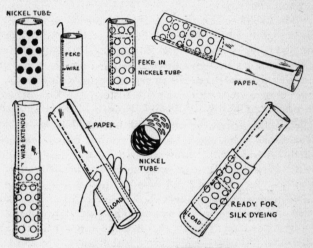

**DETAILS OF THE NICKEL TUBE,
SHOWING PHASES OF THE TRICK.**

silks are pushed into the bottom, the others emerge from the top.

The whole problem of the dye tube—from the magician's view—is the secret insertion of the fake and its subsequent removal. These are necessary to make the trick convincing, since the paper tube must be shown empty before and after the deception. In the dye tube about to be described, two devices play an important part: one is a nickeled tube with small holes in it. The other is a special fake to which a hook is attached. This

hook is in a groove, so that while it cannot come free of
the fake, it can be drawn upward or dropped downward.

At the beginning of the trick, the fake rests in the
nickeled tube. The metal tube is standing on an un-
draped table. The hook of the fake projects over the
upper edge of the nickeled tube, which is slightly longer
than the fake. The fake is painted black. The interior of
the nickeled tube is black. Hence the nickeled tube appears to be empty.

The magician exhibits an empty tube of cardboard.
It is slightly less in diameter than the nickeled tube, but
its diameter is greater than that of the fake tube. It is
twice as long as the nickeled tube. The magician picks
up the nickeled tube. His finger and thumb enter holes
in the side of the tube and thus keep the fake from
dropping. The left hand holds the nickeled tube. The
right hand pushes the cardboard tube up into the nickeled tube. At this point, the left finger and thumb release
their hold. The fake drops to the full length of its loose
wire. It hangs in the cardboard tube. The magician may
pause to turn the nickeled tube in front of a light. The
spectators glimpse the light through the holes and know
that the nickeled tube is empty. The cardboard tube is
now pushed up through the nickeled tube. The white
cardboard shows plainly through the holes. The cardboard tube disengages the hook, so that it alone holds
the fake. The cardboard tube is very long, so the hanging fake does not emerge at the bottom.

Now comes the dyeing. Handkerchiefs are pushed
into the bottom of the cardboard tube. The nickeled
tube is centered on the surface of the cardboard tube.
As the fake is pushed upward, the left thumb and finger
press through the holes of the nickeled tube and hold
the fake firmly in the center of the cardboard tube.

When the flag is produced, an assistant aids the magician. The flag is quite large. The assistant drapes it
over his outstretched arm. As soon as the flag is com-

pletely produced, the magician, standing at the assistant's side, removes the nickeled tube with one hand, drawing it downward from the cardboard tube. The hand that holds the cardboard tube goes up behind the flag. The projecting hook of the fake is deftly attached to the back of the assistant's arm. This is done under cover of the flag. The cardboard tube is drawn straight downward, leaving the fake hidden behind the flag. The magician walks forward and exhibits both tubes, pushing the cardboard tube back and forth through the nickeled tube, demonstrating quite plainly that both are empty.

During this procedure, the assistant folds the flag over his arm and gathers it up with his free hand, lifting the fake tube with it. He walks from the stage with the flag and carries with him the only clue to the mystery— the fake tube with its load of silk handkerchiefs which were supposed to have been blended together in the formation of the flag.

CHING LING FOO'S PAPER TRICK

Magicians have long connected Ching Ling Foo, the genuine Chinese magician, with the torn and restored paper trick. The trick now under discussion is a different paper trick entirely. It was performed by Harry Kellar and attributed by him to Ching Ling Foo. Kellar passed the secret along to Houdini.

The magician has a glass bowl which contains water. It is resting on a stand. Beside the bowl are sheets of tissue paper of different colors. The magician sets the stand to one side. He picks up the sheets of paper and tears them into strips, constantly showing his hands empty. He lets some of the paper strips fall to the floor. Finally, he gathers them all together and drops them into the bowl of water. He shows his hands empty,

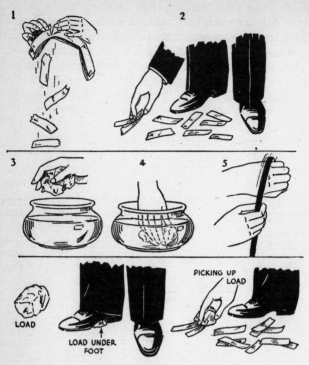

1, STRIPS OF PAPER TORN.
2, PAPERS DROPPED UPON FLOOR.
3-4, SOAKING PAPERS IN BOWL. 5, PRODUCTION OF
DRY COIL. *Bottom drawing,* HOW "LOAD" IS OBTAINED.

takes out the wet strips of paper and squeezes them. He holds the strips in his left hand. He starts to draw them forth. They come out in the form of a long strip of paper, composed of various colors. There are many yards of the dry paper.

Now for the subtle secret. The restored paper is in the form of a tight roll. The outside is pasted together. In the center is a whisk of straw, which is attached to the end of the paper at the center of the coil. This roll is previously dipped in melted parafin. The roll must be very tight, so that the parafin will not penetrate but will merely form a protective film. The prepared roll of paper is placed on the floor behind the stand which supports the glass bowl.

The magician walks to the stand and shows his hands empty. He places his foot over the coil of paper so that it rests beneath his instep. He sets the stand to the side and shows his hands empty. He tears up strips of tissue paper. He lets some of the strips fall to the floor. When he leans forward to pick up the strips, he sweeps them toward his foot. He steps back a trifle and scoops up the coil with the loose strips of paper. He wads the coil with the strips of paper when he places them in the glass bowl.

The paper coil remains dry. It is taken from the bowl with the wet strips. They are squeezed and are retained in the right hand when they are apparently transferred to the left. Only the coil of paper goes into the left hand. The magician pulls the straw in the center of the coil. The paper begins to unwind. It comes out in a long strip. Meanwhile the magician disposes of the torn pieces. He can do this as his hand sweeps downward, by dropping the wet papers on a small shelf behind the stand. He can wait until the coil is unwound, then drop the wet papers behind the stand. Or he can give the massed coil of dry paper to an assistant, handing him the wet papers under cover of the dry.

The really subtle part of this trick is the obtaining of the coil of paper. It is done in a natural manner and in a most unexpected way. Both the stand and the magician's body are free from suspicion. The paper strips must be taken from the floor and the magician uses that movement as a perfect excuse for getting his coil. Houdini's notes state that Kellar kept the coil under his right foot.

A DUCK PRODUCTION

This is the production of ducks from a tub of water. A tub is brought on the stage. It is rolled about and shown to be entirely empty. It is set in a heavy frame of wood that is raised from the stage. The frame is nothing but a skeleton stand.

Several buckets of water are poured into the tub. Then a lid is placed on the tub and a mat is spread in front of the improvised platform. The magician fires a pistol shot. The lid is lifted. Half a dozen ducks emerge, dripping with water, and drop from the tub to the mat.

A very novel method is employed to produce the ducks. The actual number of ducks is limited only by the size of the tub and the time that the performer desires to spend with the trick. The tub is actually empty at the outset. Its only peculiarity lies in two traps near the top; these may be pushed inward, and they move back to their original position when released, by the operation of springs.

The stand is merely a skeleton arrangement; but it is heavily constructed, and therein lies the secret. The back legs are actually hollow metal tubes, painted to resemble wood, and are set over holes in the stage. As soon as the cover is in place on the tub, the magician gives a cue. Two assistants set to work and push the ducks up through the back legs of the stand, one at a time.

The ducks pass through openings at the top of the legs. These correspond to the traps in the back of the tub. The ducks are pushed into the tub and when the last have made their entrance, the traps close, leaving no clue. The magician fires the pistol after sufficient time has been allowed. When the cover is taken from the tub, the ducks appear.

The laying of the mat, the obtaining of the pistol,

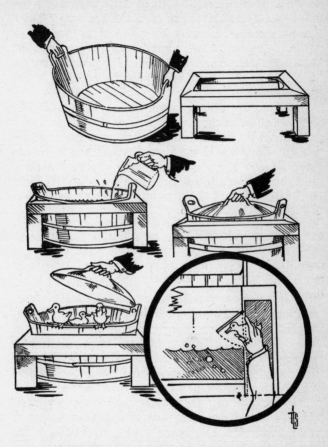

HOW DUCKS ARE PRODUCED FROM AN EMPTY TUB
AFTER FILLING WITH WATER AND COVERING.
INSET SHOWS DUCKS PUSHED UP THROUGH LEG OF STAND

and other bits of byplay give the men below stage time
to work. If the stand is painted jet-black, there is no
need to conceal the openings in the back legs. These
can be obscured, however, by the previous insertion of
an inner leg or lining, which is removed before the
ducks are pushed up. The tub is not taken from the
stand, hence the closed traps hide the openings at the
end of the trick.

It is better to use very small ducks and to produce a
large quantity of them than to use a few large ducks.
With small ducks, the loading takes place more rapidly
and the back legs of the stand do not have to be too
large in size. The stand presents an innocent appearance, as the duck tub is large and heavy and is to be
filled with water. A heavy stand is necessary to support
the weight.

CHINESE RICE BOWLS

This is a trick which Houdini obtained for his own
program. It was shown to him by Carl Brema of Philadelphia. The author was present at the time. Brema had
obtained the trick from a Chinese magician. It is a
genuine Chinese routine to be used with the well-known
rice trick. Houdini's notes state that "this is the Chinese
misdirection and the best ever used in the bowl trick."

The effect of the rice bowls is known to every magician. Two small bowls are used. One is shown empty. It
is filled with rice. The second bowl is inverted upon the
first. When the uppermost bowl is lifted, the rice has
doubled in quantity. The rice is leveled. The bowls are
placed together. When they are separated, the rice has
changed to water.

One bowl is unprepared. The other is filled with
water. The mouth of the bowl is covered with a flat disk
of transparent celluloid. The disk has a small projec-
tion, enabling the performer to remove it. The empty

bowl is filled with rice. The bowl with the water is placed mouth downward upon it. The celluloid retains the water. The fact that the bowl is upside down leads people to believe that it is empty. The bowls are turned over. The upper one is removed. The rice rests upon the celluloid disk and appears to have doubled in quantity. The celluloid disk is removed when the rice is leveled. The result is water instead of rice.

In actual practice, the rice bowls give difficulty. The removal of the celluloid disk is often a problem. The Chinese method solves all difficulties and enables the performer to show the trick at close range.

Besides the bowls, the magician uses a large napkin. This is folded in thirds. It is laid lengthwise on the tray upon which the bowls are set. The napkin's length is more than double the diameter of a bowl. The water-filled bowl is inverted on the tray. It rests upon grains of rice, to prevent close contact between the celluloid disk and the tray. The ordinary bowl is inverted upon the prepared bowl.

Incidentally, the filling of the water bowl is important. The rim should be moistened, so that the disk will adhere. When the disk is in place it should be pressed in the center to force out all air.

In performing, the magician shows the empty bowl. He fills it with rice. He smooths the rice with a stick that is decorated with Chinese characters. He picks up the bowl of water and places it mouth downward upon the bowl of rice. He raises the two bowls by picking them up between the hands, fingers toward the body, thumbs outward. The act of raising the hands to their normal position inverts the bowls. The magician rocks the bowls to and fro. He replaces them on the tray. He picks up the Chinese stick and strikes the upper bowl. He lifts it and sets it on the tray. The lower bowl appears to have double the quantity of rice.

Now comes the clever portion of the routine. The magician smooths off most of the rice with the stick, leaving just enough to obscure the celluloid disk. He picks up the folded napkin and shows that it is merely a piece of cloth. He draws the napkin slowly across the bowl, lengthwise from front to back. When he reaches the projecting flange of the celluloid disk, he grips it between his thumb and fingers and draws it along beneath the napkin. By the time the front half of the napkin is upon the bowl, the disk is clear of the bowl. The magician lets the disk fall upon the rice that lies on the tray and without hesitation, he folds the back half of the napkin forward upon the front. Thus the bowl of water is completely covered by the cloth. The whole movement appears to be a simple doubling of the napkin. It disposes of the disk without the slightest chance of detection.

The empty bowl is immediately placed upside down upon the bowl that is covered by the napkin. The right hand raises the upper bowl the fraction of an inch; the left hand whisks away the napkin. The left hand picks up the stick and strikes the upper bowl. While the clang is still resounding, the two bows are lifted; they are separated and the water is poured from one to the other.

Brass bowls of Oriental design are best in this routine. Houdini also suggests the use of a Ching Ling Foo water vase. This is a tall metal vase with a dividing partition, open at the bottom, closed at the top. When water is poured into the vase, it does not emerge when the vase is inverted, as it runs into the hidden compartment.

If the Ching Ling Foo vase is used, it is brought into the routine after the upper bowl has been set upon the folded napkin. The napkin is pulled away and the bowls are left together. A glass of water is poured into the Ching Lin Foo vase. The vase is struck with the stick and the hand is waved toward the rice bowls. The vase is inverted. The water has gone. The vase is laid aside. The magician goes to the rice bowls, strikes the upper one with the stick, and produces the water to conclude the trick.

Part Eight

A SECOND-SIGHT ACT

This section is devoted
to the explanation of a series of
unusual tests which compose
a complete act in themselves.
It is one of the most
interesting portions of the book
and has been revised from
original typewritten instructions
that were with Houdini's notes.

A SECOND-SIGHT ACT

The following material constitutes one of the most important items among Houdini's notes. It consists of a series of telepathic effects that enable two persons to present a most baffling entertainment. While the principles are not new and some of the actual effects have been shown as individual items, the complete routine with all of its variations forms a complete act in itself. Smoothly and carefully presented, the effect will prove phenomenal.

The usual second-sight act involves the transmission of thoughts from one person to another. The performers are usually a man and a woman, the man passing through the audience and receiving articles which the woman names while seated on the stage. Such acts are learned only after long and patient practice.

The second-sight act about to be discussed is of a different nature. It is of the type known to the profession as a "test," namely, a concentrated exhibition performed before a small and discriminating audience. It was designed as a routine to follow the usual second-sight act, but there is no reason why it should not be presented as an act in itself. This is particularly true because the act is not difficult. It does require keenness and practice; but two intelligent persons should be able to perform it with every variation after two or three preliminary trials.

Readers versed in magic will recognize the underlying principles of this act because most of them have seen effects in which a magician names the time on a watch or tells the denomination of a playing-card after such objects have been laid on the table during his absence. But few have ever seen an act of this sort worked up to a high-class state, involving so many tests that no repetition of one effect is necessary, and embellished with such unusual details that it carries all the effectiveness of a second-sight performance. This act does all that.

The performer, in introducing the act, discourses on the subject of telepathy. He states that he and his assistant can perform all the most remarkable tests that involve figures, cards, and blackboard writing while they are in separate rooms and not within hearing distance of one another. One committee conducts the woman from the room, while the man prepares to transmit the thoughts of those who remain.

A watch is set at any hour and minute. It is laid face down on the table. A number is written on a card, which is sealed in a small envelope and placed upon the table. A line is selected from the page of a book. Initials are written between two hinged slates, which are then locked and placed upon the table.

The woman returns. It is best to have a blackboard available. She stands before the blackboard and writes answers to everything, performing the most complicated tests with ease and precision. The act is highly effective for platform performers and when it is done as a conclusion to a short second-sight act, its effect is naturally increased.

EXPLANATION OF THE PRINCIPLE

The basis of the trick depends upon a mental arrangement in which the table is divided into imaginary sections. This system is known to both the performer and his assistant. The table should measure about two by three feet, although a square card table may be used. Upon the table is an ornamental mat, with curved edges. This is shown on page 109. The mat should measure about twelve by sixteen inches. Laid crosswise, the mat is easily divided into twelve mentally noted squares, each four inches square. While the mat is useful, it is not absolutely essential after the system has been thoroughly understood. Any rectangular mat will do; marks on the table will suffice; or, in the most advanced form, the mat itself may be visualized without actually being used. However, an ordinary mat will not arouse suspicion, since it appears to be a mere ornament.

The twelve squares are numbered, four to a row. When both performers can recognize any field instantly, they are ready to proceed with their preliminary tests. These will be described individually, with all the necessary modifications of the fundamental principle.

THE WATCH TEST

This test is not difficult to learn. Yet it is performed with such exactitude—even to the very minute indicated by the hands of the watch—that it will prove puzzling to the wisest observers.

When the watch has been set at a definite time and the performer has pretended to transmit that time to his assistant, the performer lays the watch upon the table, face down, but in a manner that indicates the exact time registered.

The hour is shown by means of the mat. There are twelve imaginary numbered squares. The performer puts the watch in the square that corresponds to the hour. Square one indicates one o'clock, and so on. The stem of the watch is the indicator that gives the position of the minute hand in reference to the numbers that appear upon the face of the watch. For instance, taking the top of the mat as twelve o'clock, the performer can indicate the number two (ten minutes after the hour) by pointing the stem toward the spot where number two would appear if the watch itself were surrounded by a dial. There is no difficulty whatever in indicating these imaginary numbers. If the time on the watch should be thirty minutes after two, the watch would be placed in number two square on the mat, with the stem of the watch pointing straight down toward the spot where the number six would be on the imaginary dial.

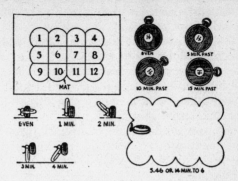

SHOWING TWELVE IMAGINARY PORTIONS
OF THE MAT. ALSO POSITIONS OF WATCH, STEM
AND PLACEMENT ON MAT.

The committee usually chooses some minute in between the fives and the performer is ready for this. Suppose the time is 5:18. He sets it to indicate 5:15, ignoring the three extra minutes for the moment; but he then indicates those additional minutes by a ring which surrounds the stem of the watch. To indicate one additional minute, he points the ring upward at right angles to the stem of the watch. To indicate two additional minutes, he bends the ring back so that it lies flat against the upper side of the stem. To show three additional minutes, he bends the ring so that it points downward at right angles to the stem. For four additional minutes, the ring is bent all the way beneath the stem. If the ring projects straight outward in its normal position, no minutes are added.

Thus for 5:15 the ring would be straight out; for 5:16, straight up; for 5:17, back against the upper side of the stem; for 5:18, straight down; for 5:19, back beneath the stem.

Once the system is understood, the performer can handle the watch without clumsiness. Upon receiving the watch, he notes the time and immediately decides the square upon which it belongs, the position to which the stem must point, and how the ring should be set. While looking at the watch, he observes his location, puts the ring in its correct position and immediately sets the watch face down upon the table.

This may be done with any pocket watch that may be offered by the committee, although it is a good idea to use a watch that is not running, for the time will remain constant and can be checked after the test.

The various positions are clearly shown in the accompanying diagrams, hence there is no need for lengthy examples. A study of the illustrations will make everything plain.

Presented as a single test, the watch is too apt to excite the close attention of the audience. It is merely one step in the entire series of tests that follow. After laying the watch on the table in a matter-of-fact manner, the performer calls for the next impression that he intends to transmit to his assistant.

It must be understood, of course, that the performer does not use the particular time that happens to be registered by a watch. He allows the spectators to set the watch at any time they may choose. It is quite natural for him to take the watch and look at it for a considerable number of seconds, since he is supposed to be engaged in concentration.

THE FIGURE TEST TO 10,000

In this test, the performer invites the committee to choose any number up to 10,000. For instance, the number 3,862 is selected. This number is written on a card. The performer looks at the card and studies the number. He may either lay the card face down on the table or he may place it in an envelope and seal it there. That is a matter of choice. The essential details are the indication of the number.

There are four figures to be considered. In the instance given, those figures are 3, 8, 6, and 2. The performer indicates the first figure (3) by the square on which he lays the card (or envelope). He indicates the second figure (8) by the pointing of the card. This involves an imaginary dial surrounding the card, and corresponding to the numbers on the face of a clock. If the card is used alone, it should be a business card, with the number written on the blank side. Hence the name on the card serves as a pointer when read in its proper manner. If the envelope is used, one end is slightly marked so that the assistant will recognize it. In this way the envelope is useful. The performer has it ready in case some one chooses to use a blank card instead of a business card.

Having put the card on the table, the performer is through with the pencil for the time, so he lays it on the table also. In this manner he indicates the third and fourth figures. The square on which he lays the pencil

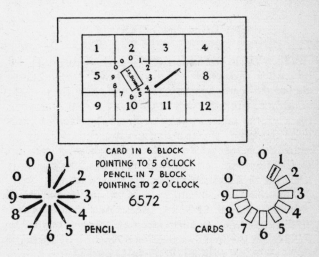

FIGURES INDICATED BY
CARD PLACEMENT, CARD POINTING, PENCIL
PLACEMENT, AND PENCIL POINTING.

indicates the third figure (6) and the spot on the imaginary dial to which the pencil points tells the fourth figure (2).

In using the figure test, number ten serves as the figure 0. The spaces or pointers eleven and twelve are not utilized. Thus it is possible to indicate such numbers as 53 by simply placing the card to show 0 and pointing it to show 0. The performer can also extend this test, allowing any number up to 12,000. He does this by utilizing the ten and eleven squares on the mat. The twelve square indicates the figure 0 in this instance. This plan must be prearranged beforehand with the assistant.

The diagrams show the working of this test; it is an easy matter to indicate other numbers once the principle is recognized. As in the watch test, the performer should avoid all hesitancy, placing the card and pencil upon the table in an indifferent manner.

THE PLAYING-CARD TEST

Another test is performed with a pack of cards. This is best when two selected cards are used. The spectators choose two cards from the pack and show them to the performer. He places the two cards together and sets them on the table. He also replaces the pack of cards upon the table. The fact that the two chosen cards are squared together is a subtle touch. They indicate the name of but one card. It is the pack itself, so carelessly replaced, that declares the second chosen card.

The rule for indicating cards is simply numerical, running from one to twelve. Ace is one, then the cards go in rotation, jack being eleven and queen twelve. The squares on the mat are used as indicators. If a king is chosen, the pack is laid on the table near a corner—not on the mat at all.

An alternate plan to indicate a king is to lay the

cards on any square but to spread them slightly; with two cards, they overlap a bit; with the entire pack, the cards are slightly fanned. This is not so good as the corner placement.

To indicate suit as well as value, the performer sets the cards in one of four positions. For clubs, the pack is laid so it points straight up and down. For spades, the pack points across. Hearts is indicated by a position of upper right to lower left, diagonally. In indicating

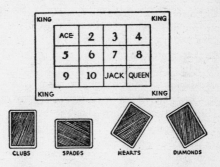

DIVISIONS OF MAT AND TABLE FOR
PLAYING-CARD TEST. ALSO POINTING POSITIONS OF CARDS.

diamonds, the pack should point diagonally from upper left to lower right.

The joker is eliminated. It is preferable to use a borrowed pack; the two selected cards may be placed in an envelope, if desired, to prove indirectly that there are no marks on the chosen cards, though this possibility should not be mentioned in the performer's talk. It is also possible to indicate a third chosen card in a subtle manner by having the pack of cards in a case before the demonstration. To select three cards, the pack is taken from the case; the three cards are drawn, noted by the performer, and laid together or inserted in an envelope. To save time, the pack is not replaced in the case; the cards, the pack, and the case are placed on the table; and the position of the case tells the third selected card.

THE SLATE TEST

In its most effective form, the slate test is performed with a pair of slates that are fitted with a lock. A person writes his initials between the slates. Then the slates are locked.

Here we have letters instead of figures, hence another system must be employed; but it is easy to remember, as it is based on the numbered squares of the mat.

The performer merely counts through the alphabet. The twelve letters, A, B, C, D, E, F, G, H, I, J, K, L, correspond to the numbers from one to twelve. Continuing, the letters M, N, O, P, Q, R, S, T, U, V, W, X also correspond to the numbers from one to twelve. The slates are placed on the correct square to indicate the first initial. If the letter is in the first set, the slates are pointed up and down. If it is in the second set, the slates are pointed across.

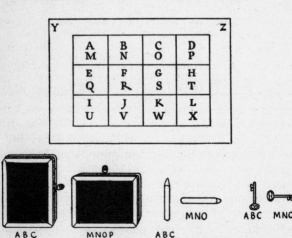

DOUBLE LETTER SYSTEM USED
IN SLATE TEST. NOTE SLATES, CHALK, AND KEY.

The second initial is indicated with the chalk. The performer puts it in the proper square; first set of letters, chalk pointing upward; second set, pointing across. The third initial is indicated by the key to the locked slates. It is placed and pointed like the chalk. Should there be no third initial, the performer gives the key to a spectator to hold. In case the letters Y or Z appear, they are indicated by placing the slates, chalk, or key to the left or right of the mat. Left indicates Y; right indicates Z.

The slates should be quite small. If the performer wishes to restrict himself to two initials, he can use a single slate, placing it with the writing downward. The slate tells one initial, the chalk the other.

In lieu of locked slates, two ordinary slates may be used and bound together by heavy rubber bands, one in each direction. A third rubber band is available in case one should break. This band is used instead of the key to indicate the third initial.

THE BOOK TEST

This is the most advanced of all the tests. The performer uses a small, thick book. The committee opens the book and selects a line or word on any page. The performer notes the line or word, closes the book, and puts it on the table. The assistant, entering, picks up the book later on and opens it to find the line or word. A word is preferable to a line if a dictionary is used.

Here we have the mat divided into tens; not units. Square 1 is 10; square 2, 20; and so on. After 120, the tens continue around the table outside of the mat. 130 lies directly above the mat; 140, upper right corner; 150, right of the mat; 160, lower right corner, etc. Thus 200 is the upper left corner of the table.

Beginning again, the squares of the mat have the values 210, 220, and so on; the points that lie outside the mat run 330, 340, up to 400. The book that is used should have less than four hundred pages. Hence the upper left corner of the table is not needed as a 400 indicator. Instead, it is given the value of 0.

To indicate any ten below two hundred, the book is placed on the correct spot, with its title side in view. To indicate any ten above two hundred, the book is placed with its title downward. Inasmuch as the chosen page will probably be a unit, the book is turned to indicate

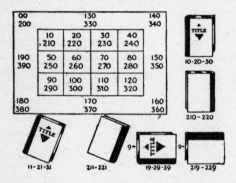

NUMERICAL INDICATIONS USED IN BOOK TEST.

the units, by utilizing the plan of the imaginary clock dial surrounding the book. If the top of the book points to one o'clock, the page number ends in one. Two o'clock, two; three o'clock, three; ten o'clock, zero.

When the assistant enters, she notes the book and in coming to the test, picks up the book, opens to the correct page and finds the line. The performer uses a simple system to indicate the line. In reading the line (or word) to himself, he marks it with his thumbnail. If the whole line is used, he makes the mark beside it. If a single word is used, he marks beneath it. With a dictionary, the performer simply marks at the side of the word.

THE COLORED-PENCIL TEST

This is a very ingenious test that may be used in addition to the others or which may replace the ordinary figure test. In order to understand it, refer first to the figure test and its method of indicating numbers of two figures by means of a card or a pencil.

The performer uses three colored pencils: red, blue, and green. The committee is told to write two numbers of four figures each, one above the other. These are to be added below a line. The addition is done on the back of a calling-card. The first number is written in one color, the second in another, the third in another; and the committee has absolute choice of the order in which the colors are to be used, for example, green for the first number, red for the second, blue for the total.

There are also three pieces of chalk that correspond in color to the pencils used. The assistant writes with

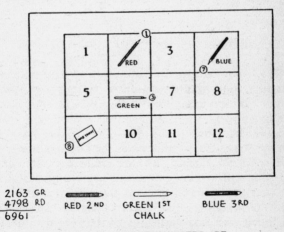

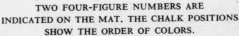

TWO FOUR-FIGURE NUMBERS ARE
INDICATED ON THE MAT. THE CHALK POSITIONS
SHOW THE ORDER OF COLORS.

the chalk on the blackboard and duplicates both selected numbers as well as the total in the exact colors of
the writing on the card.

The three pencils and the card are used to indicate
the numbers alone. The red pencil shows the first two
figures of the first number; the green pencil shows the
last two figures of the first number. The blue pencil
shows the first two figures of the second number; the
card shows the last two figures of the second number.
The total is not indicated. The assistant simply adds
that after writing the two numbers on the blackboard.
The order of the colors is indicated by the pieces of
chalk. The three pieces are laid in a row, either on the
edge of the table or on the base of the blackboard. The
center chalk (green, for instance) represents the first
number; the chalk on the left (red), the second number;
the chalk on the right (blue), the total.

This is merely an elaboration of the figure test and
the accompanying illustrations give examples.

PRESENTATION OF THE ACT

The act may be varied to suit the particular occasion,
but the following presentation covers many important
points that will make it most effective. The articles that
are to be used are lying on the table. After the assistant
has left the room, the performer begins the tests. He
should start with the slates and the book, utilizing the
smaller articles later. This is because both the slates
and the book are large objects. They completely cover
any square upon which they are placed. Should the
cards or pencils require the same square as the slates or
the book, the small articles may be placed upon the
large ones.

The blackboard is standing beside the table. The assistant, upon entering, immediately observes an article
such as the watch, and going to the blackboard, draws

a picture of a large clock dial, upon which she registers the time exactly. She asks if that is correct and the watch is turned up so that she can have proof that she was right. That gives her the opportunity to detect the next item—the playing-cards, for instance. She pretends to be undergoing great concentration and spends most of her time working at the blackboard.

With the book test, she picks up the book and runs through the pages in a thoughtful manner. She stops at different pages and still keeps on a meditative search after she has discovered the marked word. She lays the book on the table and after thinking at the blackboard, writes the chosen word.

The performer either retires or goes to the background as soon as his assistant enters the room. The impression is that he has sent certain thoughts to the woman, but that she is also depending upon the helpful concentration of the committee. After each test, she replaces any article that she has picked up, putting it on the table in the same careless manner adopted by the performer.

Without the blackboard, the woman can name certain thoughts aloud. She can also use a large slate for her writing. The vital part of this performance is effective presentation. The idea of two minds thinking as one must be stressed to the utmost.

Some performers may choose to do the simpler tests only, considering the entire table as divided into twelve squares. This is a good plan in first presenting the act, as it simplifies the work and makes a short, effective routine. But the more involved tests should not be neglected, as they surpass the simpler ones and will bewilder persons who think they have an inkling of the method.

There are certain impromptu tests that can be shown very effectively. The performer may ask for a match box, a cigarette case, a card case, or some similar object. Receiving a match box, he counts the number of matches it contains, closes the box with the matches in it, and lays the box on the table. The woman sees the box and notes that it has been put in simple numerical position, its square indicating the first figure, the way it points, the second figure. She names the number of matches in the box as an addition to her regular routine.

While the routine given here—with the additional impromptu tests—is a wonderful act in itself, many additions and variations will occur to individuals after they have performed the act themselves. They will discover methods of increasing the effectiveness of the act and should not hesitate to make any improvement which they feel sure is of value.

The author recommends this entire act as an excellent and practical demonstration of mental magic. It is one of those deceptions that can be learned and performed by two persons previously unversed in magical methods.

Part Nine

STAGE ILLUSIONS

Here is the magic of
the illusionist. In building his large
magical show, Houdini constantly
added new illusions and made plans
to build even larger mysteries.
The items in this section include
illusions that were built and
used and also those that were planned
for future construction.

This stage illusion was originated and designed by Dunninger, from whom Houdini obtained the illusion for stage presentation. A description of the apparatus was among Houdini's notes, crediting the illusion to Dunninger, who has consented to its inclusion in this volume.

A large cabinet is used in the illusion. It is mounted on a high platform and the sides consist of colored slats, the top being solid. Thus the cabinet bears a resemblance to a huge cage, through which the audience can clearly see.

The magician speaks as follows:

"Having presented a series of experiments in which I have made use of a variety of animals, I take pleasure in offering an effect with a number of chickens. I direct your attention to the cabinet, elevated high above the stage; I likewise draw your attention to the simplicity of its construction. With your very kind permission, I will present my six little chicks."

The orchestra plays fast music and six girls hop upon the stage, wearing chicken costumes. They stand three at a side, with their hands in back of them.

The cabinet and platform are wheeled around to show all sides. The slatted front opens like a door and assistants enter to draw down blinds within the other three sides. This makes the cabinet a solid box with an open front.

The six chicks hop into the cabinet at the magician's command. The slatted door is closed. The girls are plainly visible through the bars. Directly in front of the cabinet is a small stand which contains flash powder. The magician fires several quick shots with a revolver. At the same instant, the charge of power is ignited. There is a dazzling flash. The cabinet is seen to be empty.

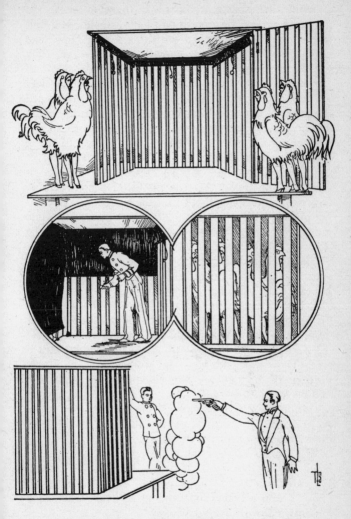

THE "CHICKS" ENTER THE SLATTED CABINET.
BLINDS ARE DRAWN. GIRLS SEEN THROUGH FRONT SLATS.
THEY DISAPPEAR.

While the spectators stare in bewilderment, the magician orders the dissection of the cabinet. His uniformed assistants proceed with this work. They take down the slatted front and carry it from the stage. They lift off the top. They raise the blind on one side and remove the side. They do the same with the other side. They finally raise the blind at the back and take down the back. Nothing remains but the thin platform, which is wheeled off the stage with various portions of the cabinet upon it. It is a complete disappearance, leaving no clue for the audience.

In considering the construction of this cabinet, it must first be noted that the platform is considerably larger than the space that forms the bottom of the cabinet proper. There is a ledge all the way around, outside the slatted walls. The blinds that pull down inside the walls are black in color.

The back of the cabinet has a door that opens inward. This is not noticeable. It is well constructed and appears to be part of an ordinary slatted wall.

It is the front of the cabinet, however, that demands the most careful study. The slats are of double thickness. Each slat is wider than the space between it and the next slat. The back portions of the slats are moveable. They slide sideways, in grooves. All moveable portions of the slats are connected by rods at the top and bottom of the frame. Thus, by a simple mechanical operation at the front side of the cabinet, the space between the front slats can be automatically filled by the moveable portions of the slats.

The facings of these moveable portions are painted black. When the spaces between the slats are closed, the cabinet appears to be empty, because the inner blinds are also black and form a dark box when they are drawn down.

The girls, with their light-colored costumes, form a striking contrast when inside the cabinet. They are plainly seen by the audience. The flash powder is the cue for an assistant at the front side of the cabinet. He

Top, CABINET BEING DISSECTED
(ALL CURTAINS RAISED). *Left Center*, SPECIAL
"FILL IN" SLATS AT FRONT.
Right Center, GIRLS STEPPING TO BACK
OF CABINET. *Bottom*, PASSING
FROM CABINET THROUGH BACK DROP.

closes the openings between the slats. The movement of the black sections cannot be seen because of the dazzling flash. The shots from the magician's pistol cover the noise of the apparatus.

The magician allows some time for the audience to appreciate the fact that the cabinet is apparently empty. During this interval, the girls are busy. They raise the blind at the back of the cabinet. They open the secret door. They step out and line themselves along the ledge at the rear. They close the door behind them and draw down the blind by reaching between the slats.

When the magician gets the cue that all is ready, he orders the dissection of the cabinet. Just as the back blind was unnecessary while the front slats were closed, so is the closed front unnecessary now. The assistant operates the slides so that the spaces between the slats are reopened. On this occasion, he performs the operation slowly and any slight noise is drowned by the playing of the orchestra. The inside of the cabinet is jet-black—the chicks being gone—and the movement of the sliding portions of the slats cannot be detected.

The front of the cabinet is removed; then the top and the sides. This is not a rapid operation. The cabinet is set near the back of the stage and while the dissection is going on, a trap or panel opens in the scenery behind the cabinet. The bottom of this opening is above the platform of the cabinet. A board is pushed through and its end rests on the ledge where the girls are standing. One by one, the six chicks walk the plank and stoop as they pass through the open panel. The board is drawn after them. The panel closes. By the time the assistants have begun to take down the back of the cabinet, the last of the six vanished girls is safely away back stage.

FRAME AND CABINET

The cabinet used in this illusion is a very small one—so small in fact that it can scarcely hold a human being.

The cabinet has thin, solid sides and a curtained back. It is mounted on a wheeled platform. The front of the cabinet is a frame covered with thick paper.

When the magician introduces the cabinet, the frame is on the front. The cabinet is wheeled around to show all sides. Then the frame is removed to exhibit the interior. To convince the audience completely that the cabinet is quite empty, the magician lays the frame against the front of the cabinet, to one side. He steps into the cabinet and parts the rear curtain, allowing a view clear through. He closes the curtains, replaces the frame, and awaits results. In a few seconds, the paper bursts and a young lady steps from the cabinet.

This illusion depends upon quick, well-timed presentation. It may be handled by one peron—the performer. The girl is in the cabinet when it is wheeled around at the center of the stage. While the magician is removing the frame—a task that requires several seconds, the girl parts the curtains and goes to the back of the platform. She closes the curtains in front of her, so that she is not seen when the frame is removed.

After exhibiting the frame, the illusionist sets it carelessly against the front post of the cabinet, on the right side. This is necessary so that he may enter the cabinet and spread the curtains. While the magician is stepping into the cabinet, the girl takes the cue and steps off the back to the stage, making a long step so that her feet will not be seen beneath the platform. She virtually comes around to the side of the cabinet when she performs this action. As a result, the girl is out of view, being hidden behind the frame that projects from the cabinet.

As the magician closes the rear curtains, the girl again steps on the platform and makes her way to the back. She is safely there before the magician picks up the frame. When the frame is in position, the girl spreads the curtains and enters the cabinet. Another wheeling of the cabinet would be superfluous. All is

DIAGRAMS SHOW IMPORTANT STAGES
OF THE ILLUSION. NOTE GIRL BEHIND FRAME WHEN
CURTAINS ARE SHOWN EMPTY.
ALSO THE POSITION SHE TAKES BEHIND CURTAINS.

ready for the appearance of the girl, which takes place when the magician gives the cue.

The notes suggest a lithograph showing the picture of the girl. This would make an excellent front for the frame, although a sheet of white paper is quite effective and does not give a direct suggestion of the appearance which is due to follow.

THE CASK ILLUSION

This is a very bold illusion, as it is performed while a committee is upon the stage. The method is quite unusual. The magician invites several persons to come on the stage to examine a large cask, which is more than twice the size of an ordinary barrel. The cask is in the center of the stage and it proves to be quite empty. Attention is called to a skeleton platform. The committee examines all parts of the platform. When all are satisfied that the cask and the cabinet are empty, the assistants invert the heavy cask by means of metal handles on the sides. The magician lets a committee member pound the sides and the bottom of the cask, proving its solidity.

The people on the stage take chairs at the sides. The assistants lift the cask and carry it to the platform, turning it so it is upright. The magician approaches with a sheet of paper, which he places over the top of the cask. A metal hoop is put upon the paper. It is hammered into place so that the top of the cask is covered with a drumhead. A pistol shot follows. The paper bursts and a man emerges from the cask.

The occupant of the cask makes his entry through a trap in the stage. The whole procedure is designed to mislead the committee as well as the audience. Those who might suspect a trap would naturally suspect the bottom of the cask also. But the person does not come

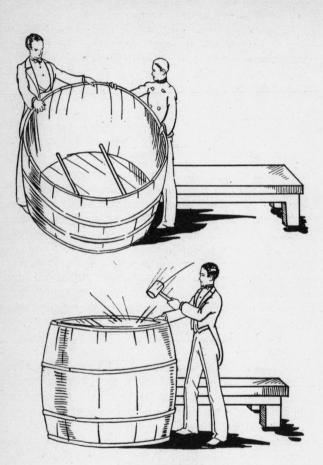

CASK SHOWN EMPTY.
BOTTOM STRUCK TO SHOW SOLIDITY.

CASK LIFTED TO PLATFORM
AND TOPPED WITH PAPER. MAN APPEARS.
Bottom, ASSISTANT ENTERING
INVERTED CASK THROUGH STAGE TRAP.

through the bottom of the cask. The actual entry is made when the cask is inverted.

There is one peculiarity about the interior of the cask. That is the presence of short metal rods near the bottom. They are scarcely noticeable and appear to be there to reinforce the construction. But their purpose is different. The cask is on the trap at the beginning, when the committee comes upon the stage. The case completely covers the trap. When the cask is inverted, its mouth comes over the trap, which opens while the bottom is being hammered. This covers all noise made by the man who comes up through the trap. He seizes the bars at the bottom of the cask and hangs by them while the trap closes.

The assistants lift the cask and carry it in its inverted position. This substantiates the idea that the cask is still empty. In setting the cask top up, it is turned away from the audience, so that no one gains a view of the interior. The concealed man hangs close to the bottom. He cannot be seen, because the cask is large inside.

The rest of the illusion is a matter of routine. The paper is affixed to the top of the cask while it is isolated on the platform and the man within makes his appearance as soon as the magician fires the revolver.

A VANISH IN MID-AIR

The notes concerning this illusion state that the idea was described to Houdini by the famous magician, Chung Ling Soo, an American who gained great success in the guise of a Chinese wizard. Soo was none other than Billy Robinson, formerly stage manager for Herrmann the Great. He was the creator of many startling effects in magic. This mid-air vanish is typical of his ingenuity.

A board is resting on the stage or upon a raised platform. The magician introduces his assistant, who is

ASSISTANT STRAPPED TO BOARD,
WHICH IS PLACED IN FRAME WITHIN CABINET.

placed upon the board and fastened to it by straps. The board is carried to the back of the stage, where it is placed upon a metal framework or trestle, which is specially designed to receive it. The board rests firmly in the metal frame, which is tilted forward at an angle of forty-five degrees, so that the entire audience can see the assistant.

The framework is within an open-fronted cabinet. It is well away from the sides, back, and top of the cabinet, which are made of plain cloth. There is no opportunity for the assistant to make a quick getaway. The magician stands at one side of the stage and aims a pistol at the cabinet. He fires a shot; there is a puff of smoke from the front of the cabinet. In a flash, the board falls to the stage. The man is gone. The skeleton framework is unoccupied. The board is picked up and carried forward. It is merely a thin slab of wood, its straps hanging loose. The assistant has escaped and disappeared—performing both wonders in the fraction of a second!

The explanation lies in both the board and the frame, while the cabinet plays a certain part in the mystery. The board is double. It is actually two boards, held together by metal catches. The top board has straps that do not pass completely through it. Its under side is a thin, highly polished metal mirror. The lower board is a thin one, which is fitted with straps on its bottom surface. The double board is not exhibited closely before the vanish. The assistant is strapped to it. It is immediately tilted forward and carried to the framework. No one sees the bottom of the board.

The framework is a mechanical device. It is supported between two pivot rods—one at each end. These are arranged so that the operation of a simple releasing device will cause the entire frame to make a semi-revolution, turning away from the audience. The same operation causes the loose lower board to fall from the upper one, which is securely in the frame.

When the magician fires his pistol, the machinery is

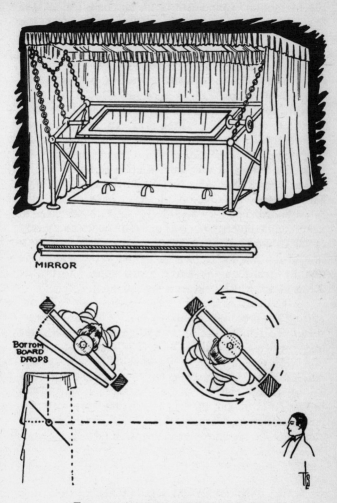

MIRROR

Top, BOARD DROPS. ASSISTANT VANISHES.
Center, DOUBLE BOARD. LOWER PORTION DROPS
WHEN CATCH IS RELEASED. *Bottom*, LOWER
BOARD FALLING. ASSISTANT BENEATH REVOLVING UPPER
BOARD. NOTE THE SPECTATOR'S LINE
OF VISION. MIRROR REFLECTS TOP OF CABINET.

set in motion. Coincident with the half-turn of the frame comes a puff of smoke and bright light from the front of the cabinet. This prevents the spectators from observing exactly what happens. The most that can be seen is a slight motion of the frame. The lower board drops as the frame revolves. It strikes the stage. The upper board stops with its mirrored side upward. The polished surface reflects the top of the cabinet, which is identical in appearance to the back. The spectators can apparently see through the framework. It looks absolutely empty. The dropping of the dummy board is the subtle touch that renders the deception perfect.

The boards that are used should be wide and long. This prevents any view of the man beneath the mirrored board. The forty-five-degree angle is sufficient to keep him completely out of sight. The depth and height of the cabinet are properly arranged so that the reflection of the top will appear to be the background. The dummy straps on the lower board appear to be the actual straps which held the vanished man.

As the board is brought forward, a curtain falls, obscuring the presumable empty cabinet. This enables assistants to remove the mirrored board from the frame and to release the hidden man. The illusion should be presented on full stage, as the concluding number of a magical act. It is an excellent trick, since the mechanical operation can be made simple and sure. With proper construction, this illusion should work with perfect precision and its action is so fast that there is no chance of the spectators' realizing what takes place.

SAWING A WOMAN INTO TWINS

Houdini had many ideas for improvements of old illusions. One of the most sensational of modern stage tricks was the illusion of "sawing a woman in half," which was exhibited by many magicians with many variations. When Houdini started out with his full evening show, the sawing trick was no longer a novelty. He did not use it in his program. Nevertheless he, like many other magicians, gave considerable thought to the possibilities of presenting the illusion in a new guise.

His notes contain the details of a new variation of the sawing trick. This material gives the basic principles of the idea, with many suggestions for actual working. The following description and explanation have been developed from the notes.

The illusion begins with the exhibition of a long oblong box, which is resting on a large square platform. The platform is turned around to exhibit all sides of the box. The box has two doors in front and two doors on top. These are opened before the box is turned around.

A large woman comes on the stage and takes a reclining position in the oblong box. The illusionist closes the doors and the assistants carry in two sawhorses, which are set in front of the platform. Each front door of the box has sectional divisions and these are equipped with small curtains. The magician raises a curtain near one end to speak to the woman. This proves to be the foot end of the box, so he lifts the curtain near the other end, revealing the woman's head as well as her feet. This is done as the assistants pick up the box and place it upon the sawhorses.

The woman gives her consent to the performance. The illusionist closes the curtains and calls for a huge saw. He and an assistant saw the box in half. The two sections are turned so that the cut ends are away from the spectators and the halves are taken completely apart. A woman has apparently been cut in half.

Now comes the surprising conclusion. Instead of restoring the woman—as in the old sawing trick—the magician has the boxes turned so that the open ends are toward the audience. As the boxes turn, their half-lids open and each box is seen to contain a small girl, dressed to resemble the woman who originally appeared. The woman has been sawed into twins!

SAWING A WOMAN INTO TWINS. CUTTING THE CABINET.

The explanation is found chiefly in the platform on which the box is first exhibited. The platform is nearly square. There is considerable space behind the box. In the platform is a compartment, which starts from beneath the box and continues to the back. When the front doors and the top of the box are opened, the two little girls, who are concealed in the platform, open lids above their hiding-place and take their positions behind the box. All this is concealed by the box and its doors. The action does not take place until after the platform had been turned around.

When the girls are safely behind the box, the doors and lid are closed. The bottom of the box is released. It goes downward at the back of the box, being hinged at the front. The platform beneath it acts in a similar manner. This enables the large woman to enter the platform. She moves out to the back; the bottom of the box and the top of the platform come back into their normal places, actuated by springs. These portions lock securely.

The back panels of the box are really secret doors. The small girls open them inward and one enters each section of the box. They close the secret doors behind them. The girl at the head end of the box lies with her knees doubled up; the girl at the foot end takes a sitting position with her feet extended.

By this time, the sawhorses are on the stage. Assistants raise the box. It is placed on the horses. The illusionist opens the curtains. He reveals the head of one girl and the feet of the other. This leads the audience to believe that the woman is still in the box. After the curtains are lowered, the sawing commences. The saw follows a regular path. In fact, the box is really two separate sections, which are temporarily joined by thin boards. There is no danger to the girls, as the saw goes between them.

When the sawing is completed, the open ends of the box are turned away so that each girl can be ready in a normal sitting position. Then the open ends are turned

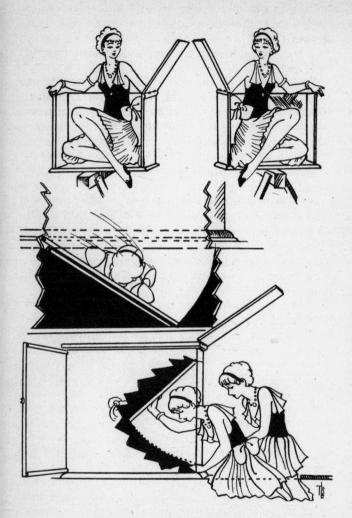

Top, THE TWINS APPEAR FROM
THE SEPARATED BOXES. *Below*, ESCAPE OF WOMAN
INTO PLATFORM. TWINS COME FROM
PLATFORM AND ENTER THROUGH THE BACK.

toward the audience. Acting on this cue, the girls raise the lids and make their appearance. They come front and do a dance while the sections of the box are shown by the assistants, placed on the platform, and wheeled away.

This illusion has excellent possibilities. It adds an element of comedy to the trick. The finish is surprising. It requires considerable speed in the changing of positions in order to produce its full effectiveness.

The box—as has been mentioned—is really two sections temporarily joined. This means that the box is not destroyed with each performance. It can be easily repaired by using new strips of wood between the sections.

Houdini's notes suggest means of bringing the girls behind the box from the wings instead of the platform, but such a plan would not be as practicable as the use of the special platform with the girls concealed at the outset. The only quick way to dispose of the large woman is in the platform; and since the platform is to be utilized for that purpose, the concealment of the small girls there is the better plan.

SARDINES IN OIL

This is a very novel stage illusion. The principal object on the stage is a huge flat can of sardines. The mammoth container rests upon a skeleton platform, which is wheeled around by the magician's assistants, so that all sides may be observed.

The illusionist steps up on the platform. An assistant brings him a giant can-opener. He runs around the edges of the tin can, opening the front and the sides. The assistants slide back the lid and the performer steps into the tin can to prove that it is entirely empty. The front of the can is lifted upward on hinges so that the spectators can see into the interior.

GIANT SARDINE CAN SHOWN
EMPTY. THE "SARDINES" APPEAR.

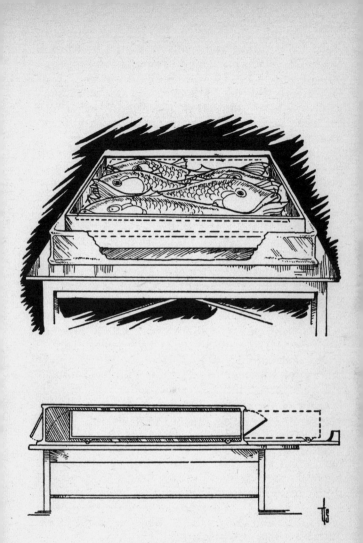

HOW THE "SARDINES" ARE PACKED.
NOTE HOW INNER CONTAINER SLIDES BACK ON TRACK
WHEN TOP IS DRAWN OPEN.

The lid is pushed back in place. A net is stretched in front of the platform, running to a metal rod, supported on two upright legs. The front of the can rises of its own accord. Out flaps a human sardine—an assistant garbed in fish costume. This is repeated. One by one six giant "sardines" arrive upon the scene. They scramble from the net and stand in a line on the stage.

This large sardine can is of double construction. It has an inner section which is really a drawer, permanently attached to the lid. The drawer has a hinged flap in front. This is closed. The human sardines lie packed in the inner drawer. The back of the drawer is the back of the can. It has hinges at the bottom so it can be opened from the outside to enable the "sardines" to pack themselves before the trick.

After the platform is revolved, the assistants step to the back while the illusionist is at work with the can-opener. He merely cuts a silver paper binding that makes the top of the can appear to be tightly shut. After completing the front and sides, he concludes his work. Meanwhile the assistants have pulled out two tracks that extend backward from the platform. The inner drawer is mounted on rollers. When the assistants pull back the lid, the drawer goes with it, sliding easily because of the rollers. The flap front of the drawer appears as the back of the interior of the can. The lid conceals the drawer and its contents.

When the lid is slid back over the can, the drawer moves into place. The assistants push the tracks into the platform. Everything is ready for the appearance of the human sardines, who roll into view, one by one.

The accompanying illustrations show the effect of the illusion as the audience sees it, while the diagrams explain the details of the apparatus.

THE TRANSFORMATION CABINET

The purpose of this illusion is to cause the transformation of the performer, who changes into another person while isolated in an open-front cabinet six feet above the stage. The cabinet is simply a box, with no opportunity for concealment, as it is hardly large enough to contain the performer.

The magician climbs a ladder and sits in the cabinet, facing the audience. The assistants arrange two ladders, one on each side of the cabinet. They bring on a large cloth and spread it on the stage. Each takes a corner of the cloth as it lies directly below the cabinet. They mount the ladder step by step until the bottom of the cloth is above the stage. The magician is concealed from view but there is no chance of his escape. The spectators can see above, below, and on all sides. The pole on which the cabinet is mounted is by far too small to accommodate a living person.

After a few moments, the assistants slowly descend the ladders. The top of the cabinet comes in view, then the front. Instead of the performer, another person is seen—in the illustration, a girl. The assistants reach the stage. They spread out the cloth. The ladder is put in front of the cabinet and the new arrival descends to the stage.

The secret of this illusion involves various mechanical details, which are illustrated in the diagrams. It should first be noted that the cabinet is not mounted on the top of the pole. It is suspended from the front of the pole. The audience does not know exactly what holds it there. The pole is hollow and a cable comes up from beneath the stage and out of the top of the pole. It holds the cabinet.

There is also a second cabinet—a replica of the first. This is beneath the stage. It is attached to the bottom of

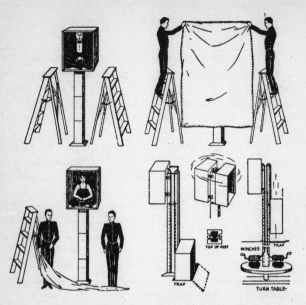

THE ILLUSTRATIONS SHOW THE CHANGE OF
THE PERFORMER FOR AN ASSISTANT. THE DIAGRAMS
GIVE THE CONSTRUCTION OF THE
POST AND MECHANISM BENEATH STAGE.

the pole, which runs beneath the stage, the base that the
audience sees being merely a dummy. A second cable
runs up through the center of the hollow pole, over the
top, and down the back through the stage. It connects
with the second cabinet.

As soon as the assistants spread the large cloth and
prepare to ascend the ladders, a trap door opens behind
the pole and the man below stage turns a winch that
raises the duplicate cabinet. It comes up behind the
cloth, traveling at the same rate of speed as the assistants. When the cloth has covered the cabinet that contains the magician, the duplicate cabinet is in place
behind the original.

We must now consider the construction of the pole.

It is nothing but a hollow shell below the cabinet. Inside it is a round metal pole, also hollow. The cables pass through this pole. The top part of the square pole—that is, the portion behind the cabinet—is also metal and is permanently attached to the round pole. The round pole is mounted on a turntable below stage. On this table are the winches that control the pulleys.

As soon as the rear cabinet is in place, the table is turned. The inner round pole and the upper portion of the square pole revolve as one piece, bringing the duplicate cabinet to the rear and the original cabinet to the front.

The assistants are then ready to lower the cloth. The winch that controls the performer's cabinet is released. His cabinet travels downward behind the cloth. The trap door was closed as soon as the duplicate cabinet had cleared it. Now it opens, when the cloth touches the stage. The magician and his cabinet pass through the trap; the trap closes and the work is done.

The back of the shell pole and both the front and the back of the revolving square portion are grooved. Behind each cabinet are little wheels that fit into the grooves. These enable the cabinets to run smoothly up and down the pole. The turntable is located some five feet below the level of the stage so as to allow room for the cabinet and the operators who work below stage.

Each cabinet should be fronted with a thin gauze blind. This is pulled down by the performer after he is in place. When the second cabinet is revealed, the blind is not raised until the assistants have lowered the cloth. The purpose of the blind is to keep the spectators from seeing exactly who is in the cabinet, although a form is visible through the gauze. This keeps attention on the cabinet, particularly at the conclusion of the illusion. If the girl should be fully revealed the instant that the cloth came below the cabinet, people would be searching for clues before the trick was completed.

The illustrations show the effect as well as the explanation. The gauze curtains are not illustrated. They must be considered as an additional item that adds to the effect. The pole is marked into ornamental sections so that no suspicion will be attached to the actual break which is necessary just below the level of the cabinet.

DE KOLTA'S ILLUSION

Buatier De Kolta was one of the outstanding geniuses of magic. He invented many remarkable illusions and utilized principles which have since been adopted by many magicians. Among Houdini's notes was a description of an illusion performed by De Kolta which has never, to the author's knowledge, been described in print. Houdini's notation bears the date January 13, 1905—less than three years after the death of De Kolta. It states that the illusion was successful at a private showing and was later presented on the stage of the Winter Garden in Berlin.

The illusion is the disappearance of a woman. She stands at the center of the stage and is covered with a large flag, held by the performer. The magician commands her to walk forward. She advances slowly toward the footlights. The magician fires a pistol. The flag collapses. The woman is gone.

The trick is accomplished by means of a wire frame which is worn by the woman. The frame is collapsible. Two strong threads—or thin wires—are attached to it. One thread starts from the head of the frame. It passes through a hook overhead toward the front of the stage. Then it travels to the rear. There is an extension of this thread that leads off backward from the frame, so the thread virtually forms a loop which may be controlled by the performer or a hidden assistant.

The other thread is attached to the bottom of the frame. It passes forward along the stage, through a hook, and back to the controller. The woman enters wearing the frame; the threads are pulled taut as the

**A GIRL DISAPPEARS
INSTANTANEOUSLY FROM BENEATH A CLOTH.**

Top, FRAME IN CLOTH. HOW
THREADS OPERATE THE FLIMSY DUMMY.
Bottom, GIRL ESCAPING INTO TABLE
BEHIND CLOTH. NOTE COLLAPSE OF FRAME.

magician drapes her with the flag. He takes care to conceal the frame entirely beneath the cloth.

While the adjustment is being made, the woman slips away from the frame and enters a large table at the back of the stage. This is close behind the spot where the performer is standing. The magician steps away and tells the woman to step forward. The threads are drawn and the form gives the appearance of the woman slowly advancing. The correct manipulation of the bottom thread produces the semblance of a walk.

When the form reaches the desired spot, the magician fires a pistol. The upper thread is released. The form collapses and the flag drops upon it.

An illusion of this type requires careful handling and proper adjustments in order to be effective. Lighting is an important factor. Simple though the explanation proves to be, it is this type of illusion that creates the greatest impression when properly performed. It is a typical De Kolta illusion.

There are optional methods whereby the woman could make her getaway. A stage trap or an opening in the scene close behind would dispense with the use of the table.

THE FLIGHT OF VENUS

This illusion is of special interest, as it is one which Houdini planned for many years: the vanishing of a girl placed on a sheet of plate glass. Houdini mentioned this effect to the author on several occasions. An illusion involving a sheet of plate glass and a girl was described in a magical publication which appeared shortly after Houdini's death, but it was not the illusion to which Houdini referred. He specified that in his illusion, no stage traps were necessary; and the trick that was published required a trap.

The author was pleased to find a description of the

plate-glass illusion, with its explanation, among Houdini's notes. There is no certainty, however, that this was the final form to which Houdini had developed the idea. The illusion, as explained, is certainly unique. Its practicability could only be demonstrated by actual experiment. Houdini spoke of the illusion as though it were completely designed and merely awaiting actual construction. It is probable that he made further plans for it after writing the brief explantaion which appears in his notes. Yet there is no proof that he departed from the fundamental principle that he originally decided to use.

As the audience sees it, two Hindu assistants are standing on the stage when the curtain rises. They are facing the side of the stage. Between them they hold a sheet of plate glass. The magician introduces a girl clad in a scanty costume. She assumes a reclining position upon the sheet of plate glass. The magician and an assistant cover her with a large cloth. While the cloth completely hides the girl and the glass, it at no time touches the stage. There is absolutely no opportunity for the girl to escape by means of a trap. The men are standing well forward and there are no wings near by.

A few moments after the cloth has been placed upon the girl, the magician whisks it away. The girl has vanished. The sheet of glass is transparent. She has apparently disappeared into thin air. The assistants carry the glass from the stage.

Now for the explanation. The foremost Hindu is a dummy figure. The figure is hollow and is considerably larger than the girl. As soon as the girl is covered by the cloth, she moves forward and enters the dummy figure. The form has no back. The opening is covered by a coat which is cut down the middle and held taut with strips of elastic. The girl's tight-fitting costume enables her to enter the figure without difficulty.

When the cloth is removed, the girl is gone. She walks off inside the figure, carrying the front end of the glass. In doing so, she turns toward the back of the stage,

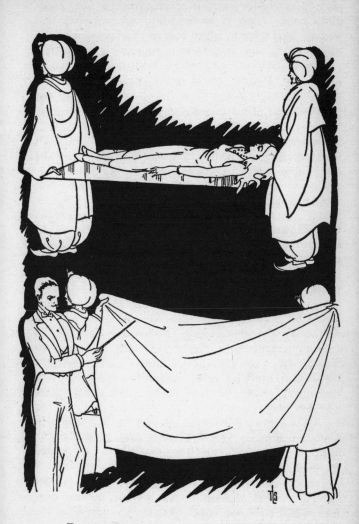

Top, THE GIRL IS PLACED ON A SHEET OF GLASS.
Bottom, THE GIRL IS COVERED WITH A CLOTH.

to keep the spectators from observing the figure too closely.

There are certain important details which must be considered in connection with the illusion. As described, with two assistants, it is doubtful whether the dummy figure could remain upright and support the end of the glass. The illusion has been described and illustrated with two assistants—one a dummy—in order to clarify the idea. The notes, however, suggest the use of four assistants dressed as Hindus. The advantages of such an arrangement are obvious. With one man at each of the three corners of a large sheet of glass, the dummy figure could be stationed at the far corner at the front. A man would be between the figure and the audience, obscuring a close view of the dummy. Furthermore, the man at the front of the glass could support all the weight so that the dummy figure would bear none of the strain and would actually be supported by the glass itself. This arrangement greatly increases the practical possibilities of the idea. With four men holding the glass, there would be less suspicion on the part of keen observers.

To make the illusion most effective, the cloth should contain a wire frame resembling the form of the woman. Her entrance into the dummy figure is effected while the cloth is being held in front of the glass. With the wire frame, the cloth can be placed upon the glass and left there, apparently covering the girl. In the vanish, the cloth is swept away and crushed, the light frame collapsing within it. There is no possibility of the girl's being in the cloth. The clear glass, well above the stage, alone remains.

Correct construction of the dummy figure, proper lighting conditions, and precise routine are essential factors in this illusion. Much of its success depends upon the ability of the performer who presents it.

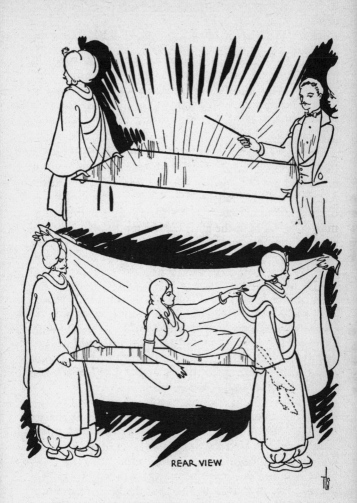

REAR VIEW

Top, THE GIRL DISAPPEARS WHEN CLOTH IS REMOVED.
Bottom, HOW THE GIRL ENTERS THE DUMMY FIGURE.

THE GIANT BALL OF WOOL

Certain successful stage illusions have been adapted from smaller tricks, while on some occasions, the principles of stage illusions have been applied to a smaller scale. This illusion is an outgrowth of a famous old trick —the production of a missing article in the center of a ball of wool.

In this instance, the missing article is a girl who has vanished in some mysterious way. Suspended on a trapeze is a solid ball of heavy wool. The end of the wool is attached to a huge reel. An assistant unwinds the wool, the ball revolving as he does so.

When the wool is nearly unwound, the lady makes her appearance. She pushes aside the remaining strands and emerges from the ball of wool, dropping to the stage to receive the applause of the audience.

This effect is obtained by very simple means. The girl is in the ball of wool from the outset. She is made up as the double of the girl who previously disappeared. The diagrams show the construction of the apparatus. There are two spheres connected to the trapeze, both attached to pivot rods. The outer sphere is made of thin wire which is covered with the wool. This sphere revolves when the wool is unwound.

The inner sphere does not revolve. Each pivot rod is hollow and contains a central axis which is stationary. The inner sphere is a strong framework of metal, open at the front. It is covered with a thin layer of wool. It has a platform at the bottom, upon which the lady rests.

She is put in this place before the presentation of the illusion. The strands at the back of the ball of wool are parted to allow the woman to obtain air. When the time arrives to unwind the ball of wool, she closes the loose strands in the back.

The ball is unrolled. When it reaches the thin

THE HUGE BALL OF WOOL IS UNWOUND.
A GIRL APPEARS FROM ITS COILS.

CONSTRUCTION OF APPARATUS,
SHOWING INNER BALL WHICH DOES NOT REVOLVE.
NOTE WIRE COVERING THAT HOLDS
WOOL, THROUGH WHICH GIRL FORCES HER WAY.

wire sphere, the assistant stops and the woman spreads the strands in both the inner and the outer sphere, thus making her way into view of the audience. It is unnecessary to unwind the ball of wool after the woman appears. Hence the illusion is concluded before either the thin wire frame or the center sphere has been completely revealed.

This illusion offers a highly effective conclusion to a series of disappearances, as the ball of wool can be on the stage for some time before it is used. The trick will prove of interest to the audience and it has sufficient elements of mystery to make it worthy of presentation.

A VANISH FROM A LADDER

The disappearance of a girl from the top of a ladder is not a new idea in stage illusions; but in the form described in Houdini's notes, it includes certain details that add greatly to the effectiveness of the trick. The ladder that is used is broad and heavy, with large rungs. It is held upright by two assistants, who support it near the rear of the stage, in front of a low, ornamental picket fence.

The girl climbs the ladder and sits on the top rung, facing the audience. She raises a cloth and drapes it over her head and shoulders. Then the ladder begins to topple. The assistants have trouble holding it. They lift it and carry it toward the front of the stage. The cloth falls to the floor. There is a scream—the girl is gone! The assistants carry the ladder to the footlights and take it from the stage.

The secret lies partly in the construction of the ladder and partly in the ornamental picket fence. Along the back of the fence is a cloth that matches the background of the stage setting. There is a space between the fence and the back curtain. The ladder has a special rung, which is the same distance above the stage as the top of

THE GIRL CLIMBS A LADDER. SHE RAISES A CLOTH.

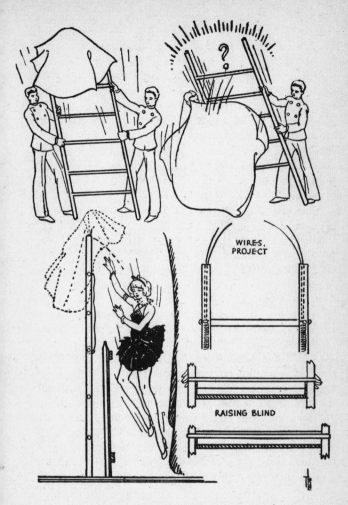

THE CLOTH FALLS. THE GIRL IS GONE!
EXPLANATORY DIAGRAMS SHOW "GETAWAY." NOTE
ARRANGEMENT OF PROJECTING WIRES
FROM TOP OF POST. THESE HOLD THE CLOTH. ALSO
OPERATION OF BLIND THAT MATCHES THE SCENERY.

the picket fence. This rung is merely a shell, open in the back. It contains a roller blind, the same color as the back drop. The end of the blind has projecting rods which extend to the sides of the ladder.

When the girl climbs the ladder, she naturally places her hands upon the sides. In this manner, she draws up the blind as she climbs. The blind stretches from the special rung to the top rung, where the girl hooks the loose end to two special catches behind the back of the ladder. The movement of the blind is hidden by the girl's body. When she seats herself upon the top rung, the spectators still believe that they see between the upper rungs of the ladder.

With the cloth in front of her, the girl draws two sets of wire rods from the posts of the ladder. These are fitted with springs and they form a mechanical holder for the cloth. The girl is free to slip from behind the cloth. She drops in back of the ladder, behind the picket fence. The roller blind and the cloth behind the pickets hide her departure.

When the girl is safely away, the assistants begin to let the ladder sway. They grip the ladder near the top and release the catch which holds the blind. It springs down behind the rung as the ladder is carried forward. Another release on the part of the assistants causes strong springs to draw the telescopic rods into the legs of the ladder. The cloth falls to the floor. The girl screams from behind the picket fence. She is gone and the vanishment seems unexplainable.

The ladder may be shown near the footlights before and after the exhibition, which gives this illusion a most convincing effect.

Part Ten

SPECIAL STAGE EFFECTS

These are mysteries of
the illusion type which are different
from the usual items that
compose a magician's program. They
have been placed in a separate
section to distinguish them from
general stage illusions.

LIVING-HEAD ILLUSION

This is an improvement on the old stage and side-show illusion of the "living head," which was introduced in its original form some seventy years ago and which has appeared in many varied forms.

An upright box is set in the center of the stage. It is a cabinet about six feet in height, somewhat like an oversized victrola. There are doors in the center. These are opened to reveal a narrow cross-shelf on which rests the living head of a woman. The head speaks and proves conclusively that it is alive.

The spectators can see below and above the head. They observe two closed doors at the rear of the cabinet. The magician closes the front doors, hiding the head from view. Then he opens all four doors so that people can see directly through the cabinet to the scene behind it. The head rests upon the shelf during the entire exhibition, after which the doors are closed and the cabinet is wheeled away.

The first part of the illusion is entirely an old principle. The space in which the head appears is cubical in shape. A mirror runs at an angle of forty-five degrees from the lower front of the opening to the upper rear. The mirror is actually in two sections—the narrow shelf forming the division. There is a hole in the shelf. The woman sits in the lower part of the cabinet with her head through the opening in the shelf.

The mirror reflects the upper portion of the cabinet. In the usual version, the reflected surface would simply be covered with a light-colored cloth. It appears to be the back of the cabinet. Houdini's improvement, however, involves the opening of doors in the rear. Hence the surface above the woman's head is patterned in the form of two doors. Those who look into the cabinet see the head on the shelf and the doors apparently behind the head.

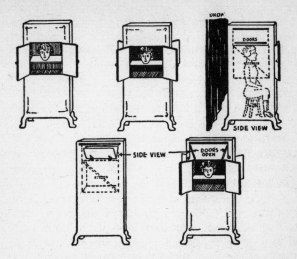

CONSTRUCTION OF CABINET FOR THE LIVING HEAD.
NOTE ARRANGEMENT OF MIRROR. DOORS OPENING ABOVE
THE HEAD SHOW TOP OF CABINET, WHICH
MATCHES BACK DROP, GIVING ILLUSION OF
"CLEAR THROUGH" VISION.

The magician then closes the front doors. In opening all the doors of the cabinet, he opens the back
doors first. This operation causes the dummy doors
to open upward. This is due to a mechanical connection. At the very top of the cabinet is an interior lining which matches the screenlike scene behind the
cabinet. Hence when the front doors are opened, the
spectators apparently see through the open rear doors
to the scene in back. In reality they are observing
the reflection of the inner surface at the top of the
cabinet.

The cabinet must be in its exact position to make
this illusion effective. The distance from the shelf to
the top of the cabinet must be exactly the same as the
distance from the shelf to the screen behind. The
same applies to the positions of the fake doors above

the head and the real doors at the back of the cabinet. Those in the audience never see the inside of the back doors, but they do see the latter project when opened from in back. Hence they expect to see through and believe they do see through.

ART AND NATURE

Magicians frequently make use of mechanical transformations or stage effects which cannot be classed as actual mysteries. This idea, entitled "Art and Nature," is a surprising effect of a semi-magical nature. It begins with a large pedestal in the center of the stage. The pedestal suddenly becomes a farmer seated in front of a tree stump, with a wheelbarrow before him.

The diagrams give a very definite explanation of the transformation. The secret lies entirely in the pedestal. It is hollow. The farmer is inside it. The pedestal springs open when released. It is divided into five sections. The rear section is stationary. There is a break directly in front of the farmer and the sections spread out to represent a tree trunk. There are spring hinges at each connection. This is illustrated in the diagram, which shows the view from above.

The sectional view of the pedestal shows the farmer and also the position of the catch that holds the front together. The catch is on the top of the pedestal. The farmer releases it. The front springs straight upward. Its lower side is covered with the artificial foliage that represents the leaves on top of the tree trunk. The spring foliage is packed inside the top of the pedestal, above the farmer's head.

The collapsible wheelbarrow is represented in all the explanatory diagrams. The drawings that show the operation of the pedestal indicate the position of the wheelbarrow when held by the farmer. The wheel lies

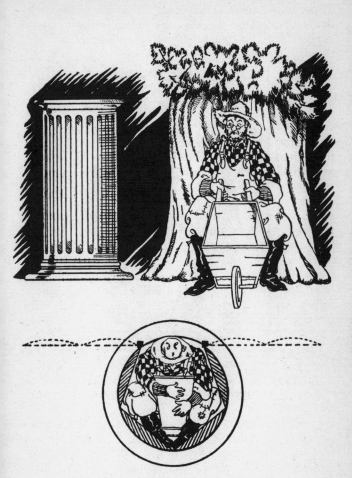

A PEDESTAL BECOMES A FARMER WITH
WHEELBARROW, IN FRONT OF A STUMP. THE DIAGRAM
GIVES A TOP VIEW OF THE PEDESTAL,
SHOWING HOW IT OPENS.

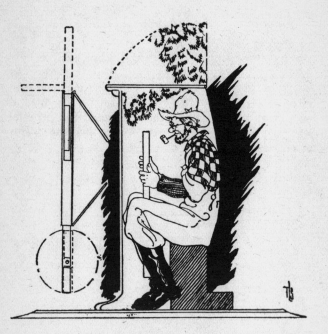

**DETAILS IN CONSTRUCTION OF UNFOLDING WHEELBARROW.
ALSO OPERATION OF THE PEDESTAL.**

flat on the axle, bringing it flush with the barrow frame. When the pedestal opens, the wheel is free to swing at right angles to the frame, actuated by a weight when the barrow is lowered. The sides and ends of the wheelbarrow are collapsed flat upon the frame. They spring up when released. The handle and the legs of the barrow pull out of the frame, the weighted legs dropping on a swing pivot.

The transformation is accomplished very quickly, as all the necessary operations blend, following each other automatically. The construction of the apparatus is very ingenious and the change of the pedestal is certain to prove a surprise to the audience. This trick would be suitable for a revue as well as for a magical entertainment.

THE DECAPITATION ACT

The decapitation act is a complete scene in itself. It involves several principles, and while the routine is comparatively simple, the performance is filled with surprises and is designed to make a strong effect upon the witnesses.

The rising curtain discloses a torture chamber. The scenery is painted to represent the interior of a prison. The magician is a grim inquisitor who stands in the center of this dismal room. At the left of the stage is a flat, raised platform. At the right stands a sturdy guillotine. It is set at right angles to the audience. To its left, in front of the knife blade, is a small basket. In the foreground is a much longer basket, which has a hinged cover.

Two jailers enter. Between them they are conducting a helpless prisoner. He is brought before the inquisitor, who points silently to the guillotine. The prisoner turns and gazes despairingly toward the stone archways at the back of the stage. He pleads with the magician, but to no avail. In desperation, he breaks loose from his captors and flees for safety. He is caught and brought back to the inquisitor, who sentences him to instant death. He is laid upon the guillotine, a framework high above the stage. His head projects from the front of the guillotine. The magician releases the blade. The prisoner's head is severed from his body. It drops into the small basket which awaits it. The assistants lift the body and drop it into the long basket in front of the guillotine. They close the lid of the basket while the magician exhibits the head of the victim.

He brings a cloth from the basket and uses it to cover the gruesome object. He looks about him for a place to put this trophy of the execution. Spying the table at the opposite side of the stage, he goes there and carefully sets the head upon it. He carefully lifts the cloth and again reveals the head. It rests motionless for a moment. Then, the head turns. The lips move. Gradually, the head shows absolute signs of life. It speaks accusingly to the magician and demands that it be restored to its body. The magician covers the head with the cloth, to free his mind of this menace. The head still speaks in muffled tones. The magician calls for the basket which contains the body of the guillotined prisoner. Lifting the head beneath the cloth, he puts it in the basket. The lid is closed; a moment later it opens of its own accord to reveal the prisoner restored to life, his head safely upon his shoulders.

The act is performed with the aid of three persons, all of whom represent the prisoner. One—a double of the prisoner—is concealed in the large table at the left of the stage. The other is a short man. He wears a cloak over his head and upon it is a dummy head that resembles the prisoner. This man is concealed at the back of the stage. He stands behind the pillar between the two archways. When the original prisoner escapes from the jailers, he runs through the arch at the right and apparently reappears through the arch at the left. In reality, he goes through an opening in the back drop directly behind the pillar. It is the false-headed assistant who emerges and comes back upon the stage.

The action is now very rapid. Constantly struggling, the prisoner is carried to the guillotine. The axe, which has no sharp edge, is released and it strikes off the dummy head. This is carefully rehearsed so that the man on the frame runs no risk—in fact a papier-mâché axe is sufficient to create the illusion. The body—apparently headless—is dropped into the long basket. The dummy head is carried across stage and placed upon the table. It is covered with a cloth that contains a wire form to retain the shape of the head. The man in the table reaches through a trap in the top of the table and draws in the false head. He thrusts his own head through in its place. The trap is designed to open and close in the shape of an enlarging circle, so that it finally fits tightly around the neck of the real man.

It is this head which performs various actions and accuses the magician. When his head is covered with the cloth, the man goes back into the table. The cloth retains the shape of the head. In the meantime, the "decapitated" assistant has escaped from the basket. The basket rests directly in front of a stage trap. The back of the basket falls flat and the man rolls through and goes down the trap. The original prisoner comes up through the trap and takes his place.

The basket is lifted by the assistants. It is turned so that the cover opens toward the audience. While the assistants hold the basket, the magician opens it and thrusts the cloth inside, stowing it at the end of the basket. He has apparently placed the head with the body. The basket may be set on the stage or rested upon the table at the left; in either event, it opens immediately and the original prisoner makes his appearance, safe and sound.

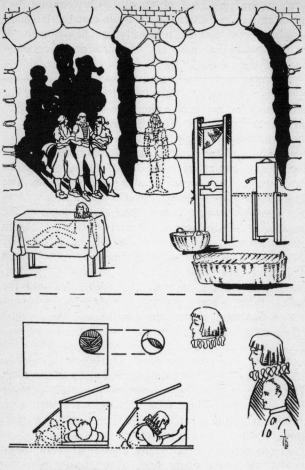

THE DECAPITATION SCENE. THE LARGE DIAGRAM
SHOWS HIDDEN ASSISTANTS—ONE BEHIND POST;
THE OTHER IN TABLE AT LEFT.
THE LOWER DIAGRAMS SHOW THE OPERATION OF TRAP
IN TABLE. ALSO THE DUMMY HEAD AND
HOW ASSISTANT WEARS IT. THE ESCAPE AND RETURN OF
ASSISTANT FROM LONG BASKET IS ALSO EXPLAINED.

There are suggested variations to this routine that are worthy of consideration. The table at the left may be constructed on the bellows principle—namely, a table with a double top, the lower part dropping when released and retained by the upper with the aid of heavy straps or strong cloth.

With a table of this type, the third prisoner is not needed. After the guillotining, the magician goes to the table and removes the large cloth that covers it, to show that the table has a comparatively thin top. In covering the table with its large cloth, the magician drapes the cloth from the front, letting the cloth cover the space between the stage and the table. The original prisoner comes up through a trap and releases the bellows, taking his place within the table. Then the cloth is carefully arranged on the table. The cloth has a slit portion that goes over the trap in the table top.

It is still necessary for the original assistant to get into the basket which contained the body. The most convenient plan is to bring the basket over to the table, empty. When it is set on the table, a trap opens in the table top behind the basket and the original prisoner takes his place in the basket.

Another plan is to have the table fitted with mirrors or a cloth that matches the scenery behind it. This enables the prisoner to come and go through the trap as he pleases. He puts his head up through the table. When he withdraws his head, he drops through the trap and comes up through the trap by the guillotine, before the basket is lifted by the jailers.

In the author's opinion, the original routine given in this description is the best, as it avoids complications. Since a dummy head must pass for the real head of the victim, the stage cannot be fully lighted; and the head of a third person can easily be made up to pass for that of the original prisoner. The dramatic sequence of the act is intriguing and helps to create the necessary illusions.

THE TORTURE PILLORY

The torture pillory is an excellent escape trick, which may be recommended for its ease of operation as well as for its effectiveness. The plans for this apparatus were given to Houdini and were contained in his notes.

The pillory is mounted on an upright rod or pedestal. It consists of three frames joined together. Each frame opens on a hinge. The escape artist places his wrists in the end holes and his neck in the center. The upper sections are closed. They are locked with padlocks, which may be supplied by the audience.

Despite the fact that the pillory has stood a brief examination by a committee from the audience, the escapist leaves it very quickly after it has been covered by a cabinet. The pillory is shown again, with all the locks in place and no trace of any trickery.

The diagrams reveal the secret of the pillory. Each frame opens two ways—either by the hinges, as the spectators know, or by sliding upward. The brass strips at the side of each frame are really grooves into which the upper portions fit. The brass strips at the top are not connected with the strips at the sides, although they fit so closely that they appear to be tightly joined.

In order that the pillory may stand a reasonable amount of inspection, the grooves at the sides of the frame are fitted with curved springs. The upper portions of the frames press against the springs and virtually lock in place. The escape artist effects his release by exerting pressure in an upward direction. He is in an excellent position to raise his head and force out the frame which binds his neck. He then attends to the frames that hold his wrists. Following his escape, he pushes the frames back into position, so that they are clamped between the springs.

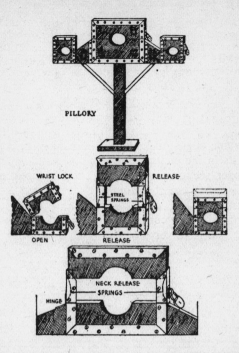

THE PILLORY AND DETAILS OF ITS CONSTRUCTION.

This is an excellent pillory escape, as it is sure and simple in operation. Most escapes of this type depend upon some trickery in the locks or the hinges. Those are the parts that the committee is sure to examine. The very ingenuity of this device is the important point that prevents the examiners from discovering the secret.

A MILK-BOTTLE ESCAPE

The milk bottle used in this mystery is an unusual one. It is of huge size, large enough to contain the magician, with room to spare. A committee from the audience inspects the bottle. No trickery is discovered. A glass top with a glass flange is also examined. Like the bottle, this shows no trick. The bottle has four holes in the collar and there are corresponding holes in the flange of the cover; but these stand minute inspection.

Their purpose becomes evident when the magician enters the bottle. The cover is placed in position and two glass rods are thrust through the holes. These rods are solid glass; like the bottle and its cover, they have been subjected to close examination. There are holes in the ends of the rods, into which padlocks are inserted by the committee. This imprisons the performer in the glass bottle. He has no way of reaching the padlocks.

The customary cabinet used in escape work is now placed over the bottle. The audience waits for a few minutes. The magician appears from the cabinet. The curtains are raised and the bottle is found intact, with the locks still attached to the ends of the glass rods.

This is a very effective escape, since the all-glass construction of the apparatus precludes any traps or mechanical arrangements. It also enables the committee to make a quick examination before and after the demonstration, while the fact that the magician is visible when confined also impresses the audience.

The secret is a simple one—another point in favor of the escape. There is little chance of the magician's encountering difficulty. The glass rods are obviously unfaked, although each is scored with ornamental rings, or circles, cut in its surface. These excite no suspicion, as it would be impossible to unscrew a glass rod in the center. Nevertheless, the rings aid the magician. As soon as the cabinet is lowered, he strikes the glass rods with a solid object and they obligingly break in half.

The broken rods are pushed from the holes. The stage is covered with a thick cloth to prevent the

THE PERFORMER ESCAPES FROM
THE GIANT MILK BOTTLE BY BREAKING THE GLASS RODS
AND REPLACING THEM WITH NEW ONES.

broken rods from shattering. The magician lifts the
lid of the bottle. He emerges and replaces the cover.
The padlocks on the broken rods have been supplied
by the magician. He unlocks them with duplicate
keys. He produces two duplicate rods, which are concealed under his coat or in the curtains of the cabinet.
He puts these through the holes and locks them with
the padlocks. Then he hides the broken glass rods
and opens the curtains to make his bow to the audience.

Part Eleven

ANTISPIRITUALISTIC EFFECTS

Houdini, in his campaign
against fraudulent mediums, designed
a number of large tricks that
would enable him to duplicate the feats
of ghost-makers on the stage.
They are patterned after
the so-called wonders of spookdom,
but are planned for
presentation in a spectacular way.

A SPIRIT CABINET

This is a very mysterious act. It is a duplication of the celebrated séances in which spirit mediums cause articles to materialize. It is produced on the stage under the most exacting conditions.

First, the performer is searched. He is tied and taken to a cabinet. The cabinet is of the simplest construction. It is nothing but a floor with solid, upright posts. It has curtains, which are thoroughly examined. A committee surrounds the cabinet while the performer is seated on a chair within. The curtains are closed. Then manifestations take place. Faces and hands appear through the cabinet curtains. Finally flowers are thrust forth. They come in increasing quantities. When the curtains are opened, the performer is sitting in the chair, still bound.

Most of these manifestations can be performed without the necessity of escaping from the ropes. There are, however, many ways of loosening ropes and getting back into them, if this plan is deemed necessary. The real mystery, however, is the appearance of the faces and other spooky forms, while the production of the flowers is most amazing.

Yet the answer to these manifestations is a simple one. The cabinet has one peculiarity of construction that will invariably escape notice. Its platform is mounted on four round, metal legs. These elevate the platform from the stage. One of the legs is hollow. It appears to be solid because it has a metal core which fits very tightly. These legs are within the range of the curtains. As soon as the curtains are closed, an assistant below stage pulls down the core of the hollow leg. This leaves an opening through which the required objects are pushed up for the performer's use.

The spirit hands and faces—even complete spirit

FLOWERS THAT MATERIALIZE IN
AN EMPTY CABINET ARE PUSHED UP THROUGH
A HOLLOW TABLE LEG, FROM BENEATH STAGE.

forms—are simply articles made of silk or rubber that can be inflated. They are covered with luminous paint. They are supplied as needed; when the performer is through with them, he sends them back through the leg of the platform. The flowers are pushed up while the performer is going through various manifestations. He ends his demonstration by pushing the flowers into view. The quantity of the flowers is limited only by the time which the performer intends to give to the manifestations.

When the cabinet is opened and the performer is released, a complete inspection can be made in conclusion. The assistant under the stage has pushed the metal core back into the hollow leg. All the legs appear to be quite solid and they are the one part of the cabinet which the average committee will ignore. This is an excellent spirit trick, as it reproduces various phenomena which many mediums claim they produce by psychic means.

THE SPIRIT KNOTS

One type of physical phenomena frequently demonstrated by fraudulent mediums is the production of knots in the center of a cord or other pliable object. It was a test of this type that convinced Professor Zoellner that Slade, the medium, had fourth-dimensional powers. Knot-tying tricks are always effective; and when they seem to be accomplished by a spirit force, they are doubly perplexing.

This knot trick is intended for use in connection with cabinet manifestations—the magician demonstrating that he can duplicate the most remarkable feats of mediums. It can also be done without the cabinet by plunging the stage into absolute darkness. The second plan should prove more workable, as the trick is accomplished very quickly when there is plenty of space available.

The magician uses a piece of clothes-line about twenty-five feet in length. It is stretched out; then the center is loosely coiled so that the ends will be close together. Two assistants stand near each other and one end of the rope is tied to the wrists of the first man, the other end to the wrists of the second man. The investigating committee is satisfied that all is fair. The knots on the wrists can be sealed if desired.

Then comes darkness. If the men are in a large cabinet, the curtain is drawn; if they are on the stage, the lights are extinguished. In either case, strange results occur. When the men are again seen, a few moments later, they are instructed to walk apart, and to the amazement of every one, the rope between the men is tied in several genuine knots! This has been accomplished without any disconnection of the ends of the rope from the men's wrists. The seals are unbroken. The single knots along the rope can be thoroughly examined. Everything stands close examination.

The method is a good one. It will be recalled that the magician coils the center of the rope. There is absolutely no trickery about that action; in fact, the coils can be made after the men are tied to the ends of the rope. But when he wants knots, the magician simply lifts the coils all together, gives them a twist and drops them over the head and shoulders of one of the men. When the coils reach the floor, the man is told to step forward. When the men move apart, the coils become knots.

If the performer's own assistant is at one end of the rope, this can be done quickly, with no chance of detection. The assistant steps out of the coils as soon as they strike the floor. The trick can be performed with a volunteer, but it will require bold and artful work on the part of the magician. He must be sure that the coils are large. In dropping them over the man's head, he must pretend to be simply gripping the man's shoulders while he instructs him to move a little further away.

The trained assistant is better, as he will respond quickly and will be sure to step free of the coils. He can come on the stage as a member of the committee. Any one may tie the knots on his wrists and thus the committee will be convinced that all is fair. The man at the other end of the rope has no chance of discovering what is taking place.

THE VANISHING CHAIR

This is a comedy trick that may be used a a pseudo-psychic trick. The outcome is both surprising and laughable. The magician shows a small platform with a tent hung above it. He calls attention to the cloth-covered chair that is on the platform. He states that he will seat himself in the chair and produce some strange results while a member of the audience is with him.

Having procured a volunteer, the performer allows his hands to be tied behind his back with a length of cord behind them. He stands in front of the chair and the volunteer stands beside him. The performer is just sitting down in the chair when an assistant lowers the tent. Immediately a loud argument begins within the tent. Finally the performer demands that the tent be raised. He is standing, still bound, beside the committeeman; but the chair is no longer on the platform. The magician accuses his companion of having purloined the chair. The man denies any such action. The tent is shaken and searched. The magician looks everywhere. Yet he can find no trace of the missing chair.

The reason is that the chair is not nearly so solid an object as it appears to be. It is nothing more than four narrow boards; two long ones and two short ones. The long ones are set at the rear to represent the back. The

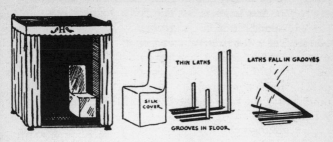

DETAILS OF THE VANISHING CHAIR.

short ones are at the front. The cloth covering gives the semblance of a solid chair. The magician does not actually sit in the chair at any time.

The boards of which the chair is formed are portions of the floor of the cabinet. They are hinged and weighted to drop flat on the floor, filling empty spaces. The magician removes the cloth cover by stepping to the back of the chair after the tent has been lowered. His hands are behind his back; he stuffs the cloth cover under the back of his coat. The cloth is quite light and flimsy; it is tucked away very quickly. The release of the cloth causes the upright boards to drop into place. In a very few seconds, the magician gets rid of the supposed chair while he keeps up a running fire of loud argument with his companion.

When the tent is raised, the volunteer is more surprised than the audience to see that the chair is missing. He is unable to answer the magician's accusations and this adds to the fun. It is a very effective spook demonstration.

This trick gives the performer an excellent opportunity to produce all sorts of articles from the volunteer's coat. This leads to further comedy. The magician can accuse the man of having the chair hidden somewhere. He demands the right to search his companion and takes that opportunity to "load" various articles into the man's pockets. This is a familiar form of comedy magic and it is made doubly effective as an aftereffect to the surprising vanish of a chair.

SPIRIT PHOTOGRAPHY

Spirit photography has caused much interest in psychic circles. Many trick methods of obtaining spirit photographs have been exposed. A spirit photograph is one in which the person's picture is surrounded by dim, hazy faces, which are termed "extras."

This is a stage demonstration of spirit photography. The person presenting the act agrees to produce a spirit photograph, using a subject from the audience. Any volunteer is used. The picture will be taken and developed on the stage.

A committee of six comes to the stage. Three are seated in chairs on each side. On the right is a powerful light above the center chair. The man whose picture is to be taken is seated in that chair. The camera is set up. The photograph is snapped.

The plate is taken into a cabinet at the left of the stage. The cabinet is provided with a developing bench and a pan that contains the necessary bath for the plate. The performer has requested a photographer to join the committee. This man goes into the cabinet. The plate is laid upon a shelf at the front of the developing bench. Other committee members are invited to enter the cabinet to assist in the development of the photograph. The curtain is closed.

Meanwhile the performer shows various cards which bear the printed names of famous persons. These are laid face down on a tray. Members of the committee decide upon one of the cards. They take it from the tray and read the name aloud.

During the interim while the photograph is being de-

Top, SETTING FOR THE SPIRIT PHOTOGRAPHY ACT.
THE LOWER DIAGRAMS SHOW THE GIRL CONCEALED IN
THE PHOTO CABINET; ALSO HOW SHE SWITCHES
THE PLATES. THE TRAY FOR CHANGING THE CARDS IS
ILLUSTRATED. NOTE ITS SLIDING FLAP.

veloped, the performer presents other phenomena in a
cabinet on the center of the stage. This can be a spirit
cabinet of the type described in this section of the book.
After the manifestations, the committee members
emerge from the developing cabinet bringing with them
the finished photograph. Upon the picture appears the
dim face of the famous person selected. The spirit form
is gazing over the shoulder of the man in the photograph.

The subject who is photographed is a confederate of
the performer. He is the only "plant" in the committee.
He is one of the first to come upon the stage. The
performer naturally selects him as a good subject. From
then on, he plays a passive part. He simply poses for a
direct picture from the camera.

His picture has been taken beforehand, on a plate
prepared with the ghostly image of some famous person. The developing cabinet has a secret compartment
in the side. This compartment tapers from the front. Its
presence is not suspected. At its widest point—near the
back—a small girl is concealed. She has the prepared
plate in her possession.

When the performer enters the cabinet, he lays the
unprepared plate upon the shelf in front of the developing bench. He stands in front of it momentarily while
he calls for the people who are to develop the plate.
The girl reaches through the curtained side of the cabinet and substitutes the prepared plate for the unprepared one. This exchange can be made later, if desired.
The plate may be put on the shelf and the curtain
drawn part way just as the committee is about to enter.
This will hide the exchange. In either case, the innocent
appearance of the cabinet is of great advantage and the
exchange can be accomplished without detection.

The name of a famous person is forced upon the
committee. In order to accomplish this, the performer
utilizes a special tray. The tray is covered with a loose
cloth, which may be drawn to one end. Under the
double folds of the cloth are cards that bear only one

name—that of the famous person whose dim picture is on the prepared plate. The genuine cards, which are examined by the committee, are placed on the tray. They are pushed to the end away from the hidden cards. The performer carries the tray across the stage and takes that opportunity to move the slide from one end of the tray to the other. This draws the loose cloth over the varied cards and exposes the set of cards that are all alike. No matter which card is selected, the desired name will be the one read. That name, incidentally, is not among the varied cards, which have too many names to be remembered. So the performer can draw back the slide to expose the original cards and then deliver the cards from the tray into the hands of the committee. This allows examination before and after the choice of the name.

The working of the tray is illustrated in the drawings which accompany the diagrams of the stage setting and the developing cabinet.

A MATERIALIZING CABINET

This idea of Houdini's involves a small cabinet in which mysterious manifestations can be produced. It is intended as a stage effect of pseudopsychic nature.

The cabinet is mounted on legs and forms a three-walled box. In place of an ordinary door or curtain, it has a front that slides up and down, so that at any time the interior of the cabinet can be revealed.

The slide—to which Houdini refers as a "half-door" —is removed when the cabinet is shown. The slide is exhibited on both sides. It is put back in place. The cabinet is turned around to reveal all sides.

Then the usual manifestations take place. Bells ring; objects are thrown through the open top of the cabinet. The slide is raised and a chair falls out. Any object

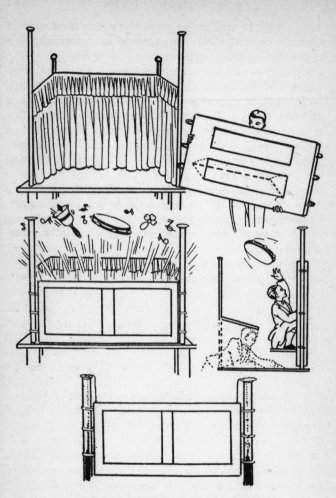

THE DOOR IS TAKEN FROM THE SMALL
CURTAINED CABINET. WHEN IT IS REPLACED,
MANIFESTATIONS FOLLOW. NOTE HOW THE
BOY ENTERS FROM BEHIND THE CURTAINS. HE RISES
WITH THE DOOR, THANKS TO THE SPECIAL
LEDGE WHICH HE RELEASES. NOTE THE WEIGHTS
FOR RAISING AND LOWERING
THE DOOR WITHOUT SUSPICION.

placed in the cabinet seems to come into the power of unseen hands. It is also possible to "materialize" a ghostlike form within the cabinet.

The manifestations are performed by a boy concealed within the cabinet. The sliding front has a folding shelf, which is not observable when the door is exhibited by itself. At the outset, the boy is behind the cabinet on a projecting ledge. When the front is put in position, the boy enters through the rear of the cabinet. He pulls down the shelf and takes his position behind the sliding front.

The performer releases the front and raises it. This is very deceptive, as the slide is controlled by a counterweight which offsets the weight of the boy. It goes up and down without great effort on the part of the performer. After showing the inside clear, the performer lowers the slide. The cabinet can be wheeled around if desired.

The boy takes care of any objects that are placed in the cabinet. He beats tambourines and rings bells. He sets a chair against the front so that it will topple when the slide is raised. He may don a luminous costume and appear as a ghost through the top of the cabinet or in the cabinet itself while the slide is raised and the stage is in semidarkness.

After each series of manifestations, the slide is quickly raised in an effort to catch the pretended ghosts; and on each occasion the cabinet is seen to be quite empty.

Houdini classed this cabinet as a practical method for duplicating the phenomena of pretended mediums, on a lighted stage.

SOME MEDIUMISTIC EFFECTS

These are brief notations of tricks which can be worked in connection with a séance, by a magician who is producing psychic effects to prove that spirit phenomena can be demonstrated by natural means.

One is a small luminous light which floats about in a most mysterious fashion while the magician's hands are securely held. This is simply a large-headed thumb tack, which is coated with luminous paint and previously placed on the sole of the shoe. The foot is raised and moved about so that the light can be seen.

The second is a development of the same idea. In this instance, a small face appears and moves about among the surprised sitters. The performer uses a sock which is pink in color. It is coated with luminous paint and made to represent a face. The performer simply slips his foot from his shoe and moves it about, replacing the foot in the loose shoe after the "materialization."

The third effect is that of spirit hands that surprise the sitters with their cold and clammy touch. In this trick, the performer must free his hands. He has a rubber bag available; the bag is filled with ice. By putting his hands in it, the performer makes them cold and they are capable of producing a weird sensation when they touch the faces of the sitters.

A GREAT CABINET ACT

This routine is performed with an ordinary cabinet of the simplest construction. It is built up on the stage and is surrounded by a committee. The person who plays the part of the medium is searched in the cabinet. Nevertheless, unusual manifestations take place under the direction of the performer, who is on the stage. These particular manifestations can be best described by explaining them.

When the medium is seated in the cabinet, he appears to be in a trance. The performer waits until the medium has gained this condition, aided by a few supposedly hypnotic passes on the part of the performer.

Then the performer closes the curtain. At this point, the medium secretly obtains a small bundle from beneath the performer's coat. The bundle contains a long piece of rope, a red silk handkerchief, a plain white handkerchief, and a quantity of envelopes. The passing of the bundle is by no means difficult. The performer can close the curtain from the inside of the cabinet, keeping constantly in view at the edge of the curtain and stepping out just before he completes the closing of the curtain. With this procedure, the medium simply takes the bundle from the back of the performer's coat, under cover of the curtain. Another method is to close the curtain from the outside of the cabinet. The performer stops at the end to hook the corner of the curtain carefully on the horizontal rod of the cabinet.

This gives the medium ample opportunity to reach around the edge of the curtain and steal the bundle from the front of the performer's coat. The performer is naturally facing the cabinet and he takes care to be right against the curtain. Whichever method is employed, the result is the same. The medium is supplied with the articles that are needed.

Now the performer exhibits a rope that is a duplicate of the one smuggled to the medium. He instructs the committee to tie it in a certain number of knots. The performer supervises this operation. Meanwhile the medium is busy tying himself with the duplicate rope. The performer takes the rope which the committee has tied and holds it above the cabinet. He drops in the rope. The medium catches it coiled and thrusts it under his coat. The performer immediately throws open the curtain. The medium is seen to be tied in the knots on the rope—apparently the very knots made by the committee!

The committee examines the medium and makes sure that he has been securely bound by "spirit" aid. If desired, the knots can be tightened. The curtain is closed. Horns and tambourines are dropped in the cabinet. The horns are blown, the tambourines are drummed. The curtains are opened to show the medium still tied. This is due to the fact that the medium is tied by any one of the many rope ties which permit quick release and reëntry into the knots. Ties of this type are too well known to warrant extensive description, as the real novelties of this act are to follow.

The performer closes the curtain and shows the red silk handkerchief. He reaches through the curtain and holds the handkerchief within the cabinet for about one second. He brings out the handkerchief. It is tied in knots. This is because the medium has released himself and has tied the duplicate red silk in knots. He simply takes the original silk from the performer's hand and places the duplicate there.

Now comes a very clever test. The performer borrows an ordinary white handkerchief. Various members of the committee identify it. The performer starts to place it in the cabinet. The instant his hand is within the curtain, the medium substitutes the duplicate handkerchief, which appears to be the same. The performer quickly withdraws his hand, holding the handkerchief, and requests the committee to decide upon an exact number of knots. This is settled. While the performer talks about the remarkable things that will occur, the medium quickly ties the original handkerchief in the required number of knots. The performer puts the duplicate handkerchief into the cabinet, immediately receives the original, brings it out, and gives it to the owner.

Now the performer borrows a business card and inserts it in a large envelope. He seals the envelope and starts to place it in the cabinet. He withdraws it to show that it is really sealed and he asks the committee to name any number of envelopes up to a certain number —say ten. The performer then carries the envelope to the cabinet and inserts it. A few seconds later he brings it out. It is opened by the committee. Another envelope is discovered within. Still another envelope and so on, until, when the required number of envelopes have been discovered, the card is found in the last one.

This is due to quick work on the part of the medium. The envelopes which he took from the performer early in the séance are nested. He also has a duplicate large envelope, sealed with a card inside. As the envelope with the borrowed card comes through the curtain, the medium substitutes the duplicate. He tears open the original envelope. He hears the number of envelopes called for and arranges the nest accordingly, by removing any center envelopes that are not required. The performer takes his time outside the cabinet while the medium seals the card in the number of envelopes desired. Then comes another switch while the envelope in the performer's hand is held inside the curtain.

The act may be concluded by any further manifestations, such as the release of the medium. The notes suggest the use of a committeeman in the cabinet, this member of the audience emerging with his face blackened and his coat turned inside out. It is preferable to have a confederate in the committee for this type of work. All articles dropped into the cabinet are concealed by the medium, either beneath his coat or somewhere in the curtains of the cabinet.

Part Twelve

NOTES ON KELLAR

The material in this section
has been selected from Houdini's notes
that were direct references to the
methods and experiences of Harry Kellar,
who for years was recognized
as America's greatest magician.

NOTES ON KELLAR

Houdini's notes on Kellar were compiled in 1916 and 1917. They were based on conversations between Houdini and Kellar and they are, accordingly, of unusual interest. They are given here very much as Houdini prepared them. In the notes, the comments appeared in typewritten form. Certain observations have been omitted, as they were obviously private statements that were not intended for publication. These were chiefly remarks concerning Kellar's experiences in connection with magic.

KELLAR'S ROPE TIE

Readers will be interested in Houdini's verbatim description of Kellar's performance of his famous "rope tie" as witnessed by Houdini. It is dated November 12, 1917, and reads as follows:

"Having been honored by Harry Kellar to assist him on his farewell appearance before the public and as he had instructed me in his rope tie, it was my great fortune to watch him in real action.

"In his start he has two men tie his left hand, slowly and deliberately. The knot is on the front of the wrist and is tied way down into the flesh, so tight that the cord is on a level with the flesh. Kellar stands there a few seconds, slowly calling attention to the knots which he has had two men tie; then asks two more to help and the way they yank each other around creates a good-natured impression. I think his idea is to get the committee good-natured, which they actually become.

"In fact, he slowly walks to the men and says: 'Put your fingers on the rope and you will see that the rope is way into the flesh.' He goes to all of them; then, when he places his hands behind his back, he does the rope steal behind his palms. The psychology is to work slowly and deliberately, as open and above board as possible.

"Kellar stood in the center for a moment, his tied left hand extended showing the knots. Then he slowly says, 'I will want the right hand tied behind my back, right up against the knot, in this fashion.' He places the right wrist on top of the knot, showing just how it will look. While he is turning around, he places his hands behind his back, gets the proper position and slack and has two men tie same.

"They tie a number of knots and in his hands I never saw a better manipulation, nor do I believe any man ever lived who could do the knots as well."

In another note, Houdini gives this description of the method used in the Kellar rope tie:

"The idea is to have the rope fastened, so that when you help tie the knot or when the committee pulls the ropes, one end is actually pulled in the palm of your hand. In this way your fingers steal enough slack so that when the second hand is tied, it rests against the wrist and enables you to keep the slack until required."

This bears out the recognized principle of the Kellar rope tie, which many magicians have imitated. The rope is first tied about the left wrist. Slack is gained while the back of the right wrist is pressed against the knots on the front of the left wrist. This action takes place while the hands are going behind the performer's back. The slack must be retained while the ends of the rope are tied in front of the right wrist. It requires considerable strength. Kellar was so successful with this trick that he could release his right hand and replace it almost instantly, showing the hands still firmly tied.

THE CABINET TIE

Here are Houdini's instructions for the rope tie in connection with a cabinet. They are marked: "Harry Kellar's Instructions, September 1, 1916." They are recorded with slight changes:

"First you call for a committee. You are tied. The Kellar rope tie. There are three chairs in the cabinet. The middle chair faces the audience; the other two chairs face each other. Bells and tambourines are on a chair. The ends of the rope are put through holes in the chair, about five inches apart in the back part of the seat. Kellar is tied at the left side of audience, right side of cabinet. The assistant takes a large silk handkerchief which is several sizes too large for Kellar. He places it on Kellar's head so it will not fall. A committee-man is asked to close the door in front of Kellar and to fasten the little hook on the bottom. There is no hook. While he looks for it, Kellar jams the hat over the committee-man's eyes.

"The door is immediately opened; next time it starts to close, Kellar grabs the tambourine and throws it up in the air. The door is immediately opened. Kellar is seen tied. Both doors are closed. The opposite door is opened and quickly closed to show Kellar; then the first door is opened quickly to show Kellar still tied.[1]

"The doors are closed. Bells ring. Spirit hands appear (through an opening in the upper portion of the door). A brass ring is handed through the window (in the door) and the door is opened. The brass ring has gone up Kellar's right arm. He is still tied. The doors are closed after Kellar states he will perform the feat of releasing himself which the Davenport Brothers claimed was done by spirits. He comes from the cabinet with the rope in his hand. Kellar walks down with the rope coiled in his hand and says that he will now perform the Davenport feat of retying himself. He enters the cabinet and does a 'self tie.' He is examined to see that all is well.

"When doors close, Kellar cries 'Door' and the door is thrown open as Kellar's coat comes flying out. Kellar's hands are examined and found still tied. A gentle-

---

[1] This and subsequent effects show that Kellar used a complete release of both wrists. The slack obtained by the removal of the right hand naturally made it possible to release the left.

man's coat is placed in the cabinet. The door is closed. Almost instantly the door is opened and Kellar is found with committee-man's coat on his back, with hands still tied.

"Kellar's coat is on the chair, the committee-man's coat is on Kellar's back. Kellar says he will hand the coat through the door and challenges the committee-man to put on the coat before Kellar puts on his own coat—after he has taken committee-man's coat off. The door is closed. Almost instantly the committee-man's coat flies through the door. One sleeve is turned inside out. Before he can realize the condition, the door is again opened and Kellar is found with his own on; he is tied in the same manner as when first examined.

"The committee-man is now asked to go into the cabinet with Kellar. He takes a seat on the chair facing Kellar. He is requested to put his hands on Kellar's knees to see that he does not move. The doors are closed and instantly great commotion takes place. The doors fly open. The committee-man rushes out with hair disarranged and rushes to his seat in an excited manner. The doors close. Instantly Kellar walks out to the center of the stage with the rope uncoiled and bows."

While this description is somewhat lacking in certain details, it gives a good idea of the numerous possibilities of the rope-tie act as performed with the cabinet. The cabinet is patterned after the one used by the famous Davenport brothers, who claimed spirit aid in their performances. The curtained windows in the center of each door aid in the ejection of various articles.

Houdini's notes add: "Kellar takes the committee-man in his confidence. He tells him to run around the cabinet yelling, etc. He has never had a man refuse to assist him."

He also states: "Kellar would have all kinds and thicknesses of rope, so when any stranger would bring rope, he would be prepared to cut same and his assistant would bring a tambourine in which would be the duplicate rope. I suppose it would be a good idea to have a double tambourine, with a skin on both sides to hide the duplicate rope.

"Kellar's hands and wrists are very powerful and he can do this trick with great dexterity. He has performed it forty-seven years."

KELLAR'S COMMITTEE CABINET

Among notations given him by Kellar, Houdini gives a brief description of a special spirit cabinet which Kellar designed for test seances and used on certain occasions. A committee was brought on the stage and an examined cloth was laid in the center of the stage. A walled cabinet was then constructed and the committee formed a circle about it.

After the stage was plunged in darkness, manifestations commenced. The stage was occasionally lighted dimly, so that objects could be seen as they were tossed from the top of the cabinet; but for the materialization of ghostly forms, complete darkness was used. After the seance, the cabinet was taken to pieces and a second examination revealed no traces of the cause of the manifestations.

As in other forms of the cabinet trick, a concealed assistant was used to produce the pretended phenomena. The entrance and exit of the assistant was accomplished by a simple artifice. He was concealed in the flies—the scenery above the stage—and as soon as the lights were extinguished, the assistant was lowered by a cable into the open-topped cabinet. He brought with him the articles necessary for the materializations. The assistant was drawn up to his hiding place while the stage was again darkened and the examination of the cabinet took place shortly afterward, after the performer had called for lights.

NOTES ON SUSPENSION

A note dated October 29, 1917, is very interesting. It reads as follows:

"Harry Kellar told me last night and, I remember, he has often related to me that Maskelyne laughed at De Kolta because of a suspension trick that De Kolta had in mind. Yet I believe that it was through this that Maskelyne eventually invented his suspension.

"De Kolta was going to get thousands of long human hairs, knot them together and tie small weights to the ends; then put them over the branches of a tree in Central Park and perform a suspension in mid-air in the open."

Houdini also mentions a suspension trick which Kellar said was sold to him by the originator. The man performed the trick on a small scale. He raised a dummy figure in the air and walked all around it. The secret was a very thin piece of glass which extended straight upward. The figure was set upon the glass and the glass was so thin that the edges could not be seen. The secret proved to be of no value to Kellar, as it was impractical for the levitation of a human being.

A KELLAR REMINISCENCE

The following story was told by Kellar to Houdini; it was Kellar's account of an experience that he had in the year 1879. Houdini wrote a brief description of it, dated September, 1916. The story is remarkably interesting as an important event in Kellar's early career. It also is typical of the many anecdotes related by one great magician to another, when they talked of their past adventures.

During Christmas week in 1879, Kellar was appearing in Edinburgh, Scotland. He had hired the Waverly Theatre from the owner, Baillie Cranston. Kellar was booked to play in Dundee the week following. He had encountered a series of misfortunes and these reached a climax in Edinburgh. His principal assistant was taken ill and Kellar had no one to fill the man's place.

He explained matters to Baillie Cranston and the theater-owner asked if his son Robert would do as an assistant. This pleased Kellar immensely, as he was not anxious to hire a stranger in his work. He knew that young Cranston would keep secret anything he learned; so he instructed Robert in the work required and the young man proved to be a capable assistant.

Business was bad that week. On Saturday, Kellar went to see Baillie Cranston. He owed the theater-owner forty pounds and mentioned the fact. Baillie Cranston had not forgotten it. He expected the money.

"Well," said Kellar, "I wish you would trust me with that forty pounds, Mr. Cranston. Furthermore, I would also appreciate it if you would let me have forty pounds in addition, so that I may take my company to Dundee, where I have a certain engagement with Cook's Circus."

Baillie Cranston was too dumfounded to reply. He had expected Kellar to pay the money that was owing; this proposal that he should double the debt was something he had not anticipated. He made no effort to restrain his astonishment. He finally turned to his son, who was present, and said:

"Robert, what nerve this man has! He owes me forty pounds and instead of paying it, he has the impudence to ask me for another forty!"

"Well, father," replied Robert, "if I had the money, I would be willing to lend Mr. Kellar one hundred pounds. I am sure he would pay it back."

The theater-owner was even more astonished at his son's statement.

"You seem to know Mr. Kellar very well," he said to his son.

"I have known him only during this engagement," returned Robert Cranston. "Nevertheless, Mr. Kellar does not appear to me to be a man who would not repay a friend."

Baillie Cranston was thoughtful. He was impressed by his son's confidence in Kellar.

"Very well," he said, "if you would trust him with one hundred pounds, I'll trust him with eighty. You can have forty pounds, Mr. Kellar, and pay it back to me with the other money that you already owe."

Kellar received the forty pounds. The next day was Sunday. In the morning, Kellar went to the railway station. He bought tickets for his entire company and checked all the baggage to Dundee. All the members of his company gave up their rooms. Everything was packed and ready for the trip. While returning from the station, Kellar encountered Robert Cranston and told the young man that he was leaving for Dundee on the next train. Robert Cranston looked at him steadily and said:

"Mr. Kellar, my father has been very kind to you and I feel that you should appreciate his kindness."

"I do appreciate it!" exclaimed Kellar. "I have promised to repay my debt to him as soon as possible—"

"It is not a matter of money," interrupted the young man. "It would greatly displease my father if he knew that you were traveling on the Sabbath. If you really want to please him, I would advise you to remain until the morning."

It was Kellar's turn to be astonished. He expostulated with young Cranston. He explained that he needed to get to Dundee as soon as possible and added that he had bought all the tickets and had checked the baggage. Nevertheless, Robert remained firm in his opinion. At last Kellar realized that it was his duty to please the theater-owner who had loaned him the money. Even though he did not agree with Baillie Cranston's scruples in regard to traveling on Sunday, it would be an act of courtesy and appreciation to conform to his benefactor's ideas.

Robert Cranston said that he would fix everything. He went to the station and made all the necessary arrangements. He had the tickets changed to the next day. He gave orders to hold the baggage until Monday. The members of the company arrived just after these matters had been completed. They registered a complaint to Kellar. They were packed and had given up their rooms. They saw no reason for remaining in Edinburgh. But Kellar had now become as obdurate as Robert Cranston. The company was forced to find new lodgings. Robert Cranston invited Kellar to spend the evening at his home, which Kellar did. Baillie Cranston was pleased because Kellar had made the decision not to travel on the Sabbath.

The next morning, Kellar overslept. When he arose, he went to breakfast, and while he was eating read a newspaper. Large headlines told of a terrible tragedy. The bridge over the Tay River had weakened during the height of a great gale. The central section had given away while a train was passing over it. The train and all its passengers had been precipitated into the waters below and not a single person had survived. It was on that very train that Kellar and his company had arranged their passage to Dundee.

Robert Cranston eventually became Lord Cranston. Some years later, when Kellar was performing in his Egyptian Hall in Philadelphia, Cranston visited him and reminded him that he was the man who had saved Kellar's life.

CONCLUSION

In summarizing this collection of Houdini's notes on magic, the author wishes to remind the reader that every item in the book has been taken directly from Houdini's own material. The tricks and illusions explained in this volume represent merely a selected portion of those which Houdini planned for publication

Houdini used, built, and described various tricks which were not contained in his notes; but it is an evident fact that the only secrets of magic which can be authentically presented in connection with Houdini's name are those which formed a part of his own collection of original notes.

The subject of magic is so broad that it would not require great ingenuity to prepare a book on magic that included some of Houdini's methods and label it with Houdini's name. Articles have appeared in various magazines and other publications that have purported to be exposés of Houdini's actual secrets. Except for those which are gleanings from books which Houdini himself wrote, such articles cannot be accepted as genuine Houdini material.

The author alone has had access to Houdini's own notes, and he has chosen to base all his writings on that material. Houdini himself collected and prepared every item which has appeared in these pages, as well as those which appeared in the author's previous book, *Houdini's Escapes*. They have been taken from the only authentic source of information. The author has considered it a privilege to take up the work which Houdini himself intended some day to perform. Hence he has adhered to the actual thoughts that were expressed in the material to which he had access. The original notes remain available. Nothing more need be said.

ABOUT THE AUTHOR

WALTER B. GIBSON, after completing *Houdini's Escapes* and *Houdini's Magic*, turned to fiction writing, creating the famed mystery character of Lamont Cranston, also known as the Shadow. Under the pen name of Maxwell Grant, he wrote novel-length stories for *The Shadow Magazine* for more than fifteen years. These novels were adapted for the Shadow radio program and today they are being reprinted in paperback and hardcover editions. Under his own name, Mr. Gibson has written *The Master Magicians* and many other books in the fields of magic, games and the occult.

Bantam Book Catalog

It lists over a thousand money-saving best-sellers originally priced from $3.75 to $15.00 —bestsellers that are yours now for as little as 60¢ to $2.95!

The catalog gives you a great opportunity to build your own private library at huge savings!

So don't delay any longer—send us your name and address and 25¢ (to help defray postage and handling costs).